W9-BGH-528

*1 8 · 4 0*

# URBAN RACIAL VIOLENCE
# IN THE TWENTIETH CENTURY

**The Insight Series**
Studies in Contemporary Issues
from Glencoe Press

**Series Editors:** Fred Krinsky and Joseph Boskin

# URBAN RACIAL VIOLENCE IN THE TWENTIETH CENTURY

## Joseph Boskin

Associate Professor
Department of History
University of Southern California

GLENCOE PRESS
A Division of the Macmillan Company
Beverly Hills
Collier-Macmillan Ltd., London

*HV*
*6477*
*.B6*

© Copyright, The Glencoe Press, 1969.

All rights reserved. No part of this book may be reproduced or transmitted in any form or by any means, electronic or mechanical, including photocopying, recording, or by any information storage and retrieval system, without permission in writing from the Publisher.

First printing, 1969.

Library of Congress catalog card number: 78-75964

Glencoe Press.
A Division of The Macmillan Company.

Printed in the United States of America.

Collier-Macmillan Canada, Ltd., Toronto, Canada.

# Preface

> The problem of the twentieth century
> is the problem of the color-line, —
> the relation of the darker to the lighter
> races of men in Asia and Africa, in
> America . . . .
>
> —W. E. B. Du Bois, *The Souls of Black Folk* (1903)

One of the most persistent themes in American social history has been the estrangement between the races. Beginning with the establishment of slavery in the seventeenth century and continuing with the development of Jim Crow legislative policies in the nineteenth and twentieth centuries, Negroes and other ethnic groups have been the objects of discrimination, injustice, and violent onslaughts by Caucasians. Segregated, beaten, lynched, and morally violated, the darker races—the Black man in particular—have been victimized by a society imbued with racist attitudes and feelings.

The conflict between the racial ethnic groups in the twentieth century has intensified with their demographic proximity. The dimensions of contact, once set within a more clearly defined legal, economic, and political context, have been challenged and changed in the large and small urban centers of America. Increasing industrialism, two major and several minor wars, mechanization of the farms, immigration, and other factors have brought Caucasian-, Negro-, Mexican-, Japanese-, and Puerto Rican-Americans into close contact with one another. The historical and continuing unwillingness, or inability, of the Caucasian to regard members of other racial and ethnic groups as equal participants in a social structure has led to group violence.

This volume of the Insight Series deals with conflict between the races as expressed in two forms of violence: the urban racial riot and the racial protest riot. The division of the book signifies the two distinct manifestations of conflict which have occurred in the twentieth century.

The first part of the book analyzes the causes and nature of the race riot as a form of Caucasian aggression. The race riot was invariably begun by marauding Whites who invaded the fringes of the minority-group communities. The second part of the book concentrates on the protest riot. Beginning in 1964, the ghetto communities in the major and minor cities of the North and West rose up in frustration and anger and retaliated against the racism they had long endured.

ALMA COLLEGE
MONTEITH LIBRARY
ALMA, MICHIGAN

Clearly, the race riots of the first four decades of the century were determining factors in producing the protest revolt of the sixties. Other causes which produced the explosion of the ghetto areas are explored in the second section of the work. The words of the poet Langston Hughes in the 1920's, however, signaled its coming:*

> Negroes,
> Sweet and docile,
> Meek, humble and kind:
> Beware the day
> They change their minds!

The race riots that raged from 1906 to 1943 occurred because Whites felt the license to prove their domination and superiority over Blacks. The protest riots of the 1960's occurred because Negroes were eager to overthrow that domination and to prove their equality and dignity. Thus, the first form of riot reflects the extension of racism; the second reflects the response to that racism.

J. B.

Los Angeles, California
September, 1968

---

* Copyright 1948 by Alfred A. Knopf, Inc. Reprinted from *Selected Poems*, by Langston Hughes, by permission of the publisher.

(NOTE.—Throughout this book, the author–editor's footnotes are marked by symbols— *, †—and the original quoted notes by numerals.

The author wishes to express his deep appreciation for the editorial assistance rendered by Miss Catherine Braun in the preparation of this volume.)

# CONTENTS

## Part One: Race Riots

## Part Two: Protest Riots

# PART ONE

# RACE RIOTS

Violence against Negro and other ethnic groups has been an integral part of the history of race relations in the United States, the most serious forms of violence being the riot and the lynching. Each involves mob actions; each draws its motivation from conscious and subconscious prejudices.

In the context of mob activities, prejudice is a pattern of hostility directed against a specific group or an individual who represents the group. Prejudice is based on the presumed inferiority of others, an assumption that receives its strength from irrational sources and frequently expresses itself in wrathful actions of a verbal and physical nature.

In America, the race riot has been a primary channel of White aggression. Indeed, mob action against the Negro can be traced back to the eighteenth century when marauding Whites stormed into Negro sections in northern communities, burned and looted homes and businesses, physically assaulted men, women, and children—all with impunity from the law-enforcement agencies of society.

During periods of national stress, hostilities toward minority groups operate on a surface level and often erupt with the slightest provocation. The intense decade of the 1860's was such a time. Fearful of job competition from free Blacks, anticipating that emancipation of the slaves would cause the depression of wages and the employment market, distrustful of Negroes because of alleged immoralities and angered over the use of Negroes as strikebreakers, White laborers attacked Negroes in many northern and midwestern areas. Race riots occurred in Chicago, Detroit, Cleveland, Buffalo, Philadelphia, Boston, New York, and in other smaller cities. The worst outbreak took place in New York City in 1863 soon after the passage of the Conscription Act. Both employed and unemployed workers, mainly from the lower classes, fell upon Negroes in the city and in the borough of Brooklyn with a ferocity that caused many Negroes, in the words of a contemporary account, to be "killed and thrown into the rivers, a great number hung to trees and lampposts, numbers shot down." The riot was quelled after four frenetic days of destruction.

The initiation of a riot is based upon preconditioned assumptions about the group being assaulted. The etiology of riots, however, also reveals other factors that cause their eruption. As psychologist Gordon W. Allport in *The Nature of Prejudice* wrote of the origins of riots:

> Most riots occur where there has been some rapid change in the prevailing social situation. There has been an "invasion" of a residential district by Negroes, or members of a certain ethnic group have been imported as strikebreakers in a region of industrial unrest, or there has been a rapid rise in immigrant population in an unstable region. None of these conditions alone produces riots. There must also be a prepared ground of previous hostility and well-formed ideas concerning the "menace" of the particular group that is attacked.*

The race riots that have occurred in the twentieth century have generally conformed to the type of aggressive mob actions of Caucasians of the previous centuries. Nine major riots are analyzed in the first division of this book. Of the nine, seven were race riots. All were caused by a multiplicity of factors; however, certain patterns of the riots do emerge:

1) The most important variable appears to be that of the aggressor group. Regardless of the immediate causative factors which initiated the riots, their character was essentially determined by the race of the attackers. In each of the seven race riots, it was the White group who sparked the incident by attacking members of the minority group.

By contrast, two riots which occurred during the same period—the Harlem Riots of 1935 and 1943—were initiated by Negroes but assumed a different form of development. In both of these riots, White and Black mobs did not clash. Rather, Negroes vented their frustration on ghetto businesses, White policemen, and Whites who chanced to be within the area at the time. The violence was confined to the ghetto community.

2) In the majority of the riots, some extraordinary social condition prevailed at the time of the outbreak: prewar changes, wartime mobility, postwar adjustment, or economic depression.

3) Extenuating social conditions were intensified by climatic factors. The majority of the riots occurred during the hot and humid summer months. Increased numbers of young people were out of school, and these and others took to the streets to find relief from heat and boredom. The result was a large, idle population upon which a riot could draw.

4) The role of rumor was extremely important in reinforcing the prior assumptions held about the group being assaulted. The frequency with which exaggerated versions of events or wholly fabricated stories were spreading

---

* Gordon W. Allport, *The Nature of Prejudice* (New York: Doubleday & Co., 1954), p. 59.

contributed to strong antagonisms. All types of misdeeds and foulness were attributed to the minority group: robbery, attack, rape, conspiracy, and vileness. Rumor apparently played an important role at every stage of the riot build-up. Rumor preceded the initial attack by the majority with various stories which heightened ethnic tensions. During the violence rumors in the form of alleged sins perpetuated the actions of the mobs, particularly by the aggressors. In each case the incident which preceded the riots—that is, a robbery or physical abuse of or by a single member of the non-White group—was sufficient to justify the acts of the majority.

5) More than any other institution, the police force was invariably involved either as a precipitating cause or as a perpetuating factor in the riots. In almost every one of the riots, the police sided with the attackers, either by actually participating in, or by failing to quell, the attack.

6) Finally, in almost every instance, the fighting occurred within the fringes of the minority-group community, thereby causing considerable damage in the area which could least afford it.

In the final analysis, the race riots of the twentieth century have been the product of a society desirous of maintaining its superiority over racial and ethnic minorities, of venting its frustrations in times of distress, of attacking those least able to defend themselves.

# Chapter One

# Race Prejudice:
# The Fear of Racial Impurity

The prevailing racist attitudes of Americans in the period preceding the Civil War were noted by Alexis de Toqueville in his classic, *Democracy in America*, the first comprehensive, perceptive examination of the political and social institutions, and of the manners and mores of the people of the United States. The prejudices of American Caucasions regarding Negroes and Indians explain the riots that occurred in the preceding century and forecast those that would continue into the mid-forties of the next century.

The earliest major race riots of the twentieth century—Springfield, Ohio and Atlanta in 1906 and Springfield, Illinois, in 1908—reflected the same deep-rooted prejudices. Basic to the whole fabric of racial prejudice in the United States is the conception of the Black man as a "savage" with an accompanying mythology about his behavior. One of the most persistent is the myth which holds that the Negro is an extraordinary sexual being. This myth projects both Black men and women as most desirous sexual partners and projects even further that the Black man is especially coveteous of the White woman. In this three-way combination, the Negro constitutes a never-ending menace to the "purity" of the White race. The protection of the sanctity of White women became an obsession among Whites. As Gunnar Myrdal wrote in his outstanding work on race relations in the United States, *An American Dilemma:* "Sexual association itself is punished by death and is accompanied by tremendous public excitement."* To prevent sexual union was to curtail intermarriage; and this explains the actions on the part of Caucasions to punish severely any overt or alleged act transgressing the taboos of sex between the races.

Although the causes of the three riots in the years 1906 and 1908 were multiple—in the Springfield riot of 1908, for example, tension was created as a result of Negro migrations and competition for jobs—one of the most important underlying causes was circulating tales of sexual molestations. In Atlanta during the week prior to the riot, newspapers vividly chronicled attacks by Negroes on White women. On the Saturday before the riot broke out, the *Atlanta Extra* issued four extras relating four separate sexual assaults, some valid, others fictional. Four days of rioting ensued. In both of the Springfield riots, the spark which ignited the actions was the traditional story of the violation of a White woman. Both riots are examples of the social bitterness and brutality that is the response to unsubstantiated rumor or deliberate falsehoods based on preconceived prejudices. The Chicago Commission on Race Relations related after their study of the 1908 affair: "Not until the damage had been done, was its falsity confessed by the woman who told it."

All three riots involved large-scale terrorism and lawlessness with indiscriminate attacks on Negroes and destruction of their homes and businesses. In general, Negroes did not retaliate against White mobs but withstood the violence by protecting themselves as well as possible.

# The Inequality of Races in America (1835)†

*Alexis de Tocqueville*

Alexis de Tocqueville was requested by the French government in 1831 to visit the United States and report on our prisons and penitentiaries. Upon his return to his native country, he wrote *Democracy in America*, which was published in 1835 and again in 1840. De Tocqueville's observations, analyses, and conclusions about the nature of American society of the period and nature

---

* Gunnar Myrdal, *An American Dilemma* (New York: Harper & Bros., 1944), p. 587.

† From *Democracy in America* by Alexis de Tocqueville, trans. by Phillips Bradley. Copyright 1945 by Alfred A. Knopf, Inc. Reprinted by permission of the publisher.

of change within the society have proven to be remarkably accurate and in-
sightful. This passage is from the chapter called "The Three Races in the
United States."

I see that in a certain portion of the territory of the United States
at the present day the legal barrier which separated the two races is
falling away, but not that which exists in the manners of the country;
slavery recedes, but the prejudice to which it has given birth is im-
movable. Whoever has inhabited the United States must have perceived
that in those parts of the Union in which the Negroes are no longer
slaves they have in no wise drawn nearer to the Whites. On the contrary, the prejudice of race appears to be stronger in the states that
have abolished slavery than in those where it still exists; and nowhere
is it so intolerant as in those states where servitude has never been
known.

It is true that in the North of the Union marriages may be legally
contracted between Negroes and Whites; but public opinion would
stigmatize as infamous a man who should connect himself with a
Negress, and it would be difficult to cite a single instance of such a
union. The electoral franchise has been conferred upon the Negroes
in almost all the states in which slavery has been abolished, but if they
come forward to vote, their lives are in danger. If oppressed, they may
bring an action at law, but they will find none but Whites among their
judges; and although they may legally serve as jurors, prejudice repels
them from that office. The same schools do not receive the children
of the Black and of the European. In the theaters gold cannot procure
a seat for the servile race beside their former masters; in the hospitals
they lie apart; and although they are allowed to invoke the same God
as the Whites, it must be at a different altar and in their own churches,
with their own clergy. The gates of heaven are not closed against them,
but their inferiority is continued to the very confines of the other world.
When the Negro dies, his bones are cast aside, and the distinction of
condition prevails even in the equality of death. Thus the Negro is
free, but he can share neither the rights, nor the pleasures, nor the
labor, nor the afflictions, nor the tomb of him whose equal he has been
declared to be; and he cannot meet him upon fair terms in life or in
death.

In the South, where slavery still exists, the Negroes are less carefully
kept apart; they sometimes share the labors and the recreations of
the Whites; the Whites consent to intermix with them to a certain

extent, and although legislation treats them more harshly, the habits of the people are more tolerant and compassionate. In the South the master is not afraid to raise his slave to his own standing, because he knows that he can in a moment reduce him to the dust at pleasure. In the North the White no longer distinctly perceives the barrier that separates him from the degraded race, and he shuns the Negro with the more pertinacity since he fears lest they should some day be confounded together.

Among the Americans of the South, Nature sometimes reasserts her rights and restores a transient equality between the Blacks and the Whites; but in the North pride restrains the most imperious of human passions. The American of the northern states would perhaps allow the Negress to share his licentious pleasures if the laws of his country did not declare that she may aspire to be the legitimate partner of his bed, but he recoils with horror from her who might become his wife.

Thus it is in the United States that the prejudice which repels the Negroes seems to increase in proportion as they are emancipated, and inequality is sanctioned by the manners while it is effaced from the laws of the country. But if the relative position of the two races that inhabit the United States is such as I have described, why have the Americans abolished slavery in the North of the Union, why do they maintain it in the South, and why do they aggravate its hardships? The answer is easily given. It is not for the good of the Negroes, but for that of the Whites, that measures are taken to abolish slavery in the United States.

## The Mob at Springfield, Ohio (1906)*

Springfield is a city of about 40,000 inhabitants, forty-five miles west of Columbus, and is a railroad center, where three important lines cross. It has had a dark record for a previous lynching, so that the unruly and vagrant element knew how to flout the law when the occasion arose. The crime was one to stir the passions of lawless men— the stabbing and probable murder of a railroad man by two Negroes.

---

* *The Independent* (March 8, 1906), 582–584.

The angry crowd were ready to lynch the criminals, and would have speedily done it if they had got the chance; but the sheriff took the men out of town, and the mob then wreaked their vengeance on perfectly innocent people. It is a way mobs have of doing. They cannot reason or distinguish. They are mad with passion, which must be vented on somebody. So, in this case, not being able to hang, or shoot, or burn the men they wanted, they attacked the Negro quarter of the city, the drinking holes and the congested slums, and set fire to them, driving out the inhabitants. . . . Then the authorities got the upper hand. The Governor called out the militia, and the attempt on the second night to repeat the outrages of the first night was a failure. The assailants were driven back and scattered wherever they tried to gather, and arrests were made, and those who resisted the police were fined and punished. Then the usual order reigned, and the sound, worthy citizens protested, somewhat too late, that mobs ought not to murder, and that it was wrong to do wrong; a tardy and ineffective conclusion, to be sure, but about all they could then do after the event.

That such a murderous mob could be gathered in the town that boasts of churches and Heidelberg College, that has public schools and a public library, is very sad and strange. It shows what a large number of our people, of men who vote and make our laws, have no respect for law, or no faith in law. They were ready, hundreds of them, to overturn law, and take the execution of punishment in their own hands. When thwarted by the officers of law, they were ready to strike and burn and kill where they could. They are—or were for the time—simply a band of savages, who had left civilization behind them. But we rejoice greatly that the authorities were too strong for the mob. They protected the prisoners, and they restored order vigorously as soon as possible, and have begun to punish the leaders. That is, so far, a credit to the city of Springfield and the state of Ohio, and especially its governor. It is to the credit of their firmness that, when next New Year the lynchings are tabulated, Ohio will bear a clean record. There are states in which law is less honored, and where the sheriffs often fail to protect their arrested criminals; but Ohio, as yet, stands with a pure record for the year.

We hardly need to say that, while lynching is bad everywhere, it is most to be condemned in these northern states. Here public sentiment is most against it. Here we pretend to try to give at least his equal legal rights to the Negro. We do not forbid him to vote, or to ride in the public conveyances, or to enjoy the ordinary rights of human beings.

We claim to believe in liberty, fraternity and equality. We condemn
the race-spirit and the race-discrimination in the southern states. This
is a part of our idea of civilization and of liberty. There is no excuse for
us if we lynch any man, White or black, for our laws will serve out
justice to him.

We must hope and believe that it is a crank of a member who has
introduced into the Mississippi Legislature a bill to make lynching
easy and safe. To be sure, he is the brother of a United States Senator
from Mississippi, but a good man may have a bad brother. The bill
provides that lynching shall not be classed as murder or manslaughter,
and that it shall be left to the jury, in case a man is convicted for
lynching, to fix the punishment. That would usually liberate any one
accused, as the jury could be depended upon not to agree upon anything
radical or disagreeable. The jury would represent the community that
did the lynching. But we are slow to believe that such a bill could
become a law. . . . The law must be held straight to the standard of
right, even if not well enforced. Mobs may arise in any city—we have
had murderous mobs in New York; but laws and courts must be the
protection of the state.

# An American Kishinev (1906)*

The city of Atlanta, Georgia, was disgraced on Saturday and Sunday
by riots of White men against the Negro population. Temporarily
civilization was suspended. For brutality and wanton cruelty and
fiendish rage and indiscriminate savagery one would have to turn to
accounts of massacres in Russia or Turkey for a parallel. Ten Negroes
are known to have been killed; how many more can only be surmised.
The known deaths of White people are said to have been not more
than two. The wounded, some of them injured mortally, are reported
to number seven score or more. No one, not even those in the city itself,
has any means of knowing what all the casualties have amounted to.

The riots are a culmination of conditions in Atlanta which have
been growing for weeks more and more tense. The recent campaign

---

* *The Outlook* (September 29, 1906), 241–242. Kishinev, in Bessarabia, was the
site, in 1903, of a dreadful pogrom incited by reports of Jewish ritual murder.

for the governorship raised the race issue to undue prominence. At the same time, in Atlanta, unprotected White women have suffered at the hands of several Negro brutes. The race feeling, which is acuter in Atlanta than in almost any other southern city, has been inflamed by these occurrences. In particular, one newspaper, the *Atlanta News*, has deliberately and continually roused race hatred and rancor. On Friday a Negro assailant was on trial, when the father of the injured girl asked the recorder's permission to let him deal with the Negro before him with his own hands. An outbreak was threatened and barely averted there in open court. On the same day another Negro, held on the charge of attempting the same offense, was almost lynched in front of the police barracks. On Saturday the late editions of the evening papers announced the commission of three more such crimes by Negroes.

Immediately the cry against the Negroes was raised in the streets; mobs of White men gathered; Negroes fled the streets. Wherever a colored man was seen he was attacked. The mobs closed in upon the trolley cars and dragged the colored passengers, unprepared for the onslaught, from their seats. A riotous crowd broke into a shop where there were two Negro barbers, beat them to death and mangled their bodies. One Negro was killed in the shadow of a monument; another was stabbed to death on the post-office steps. The Governor mobilized the militia, but the mobs, taking it for granted that the militiamen were in sympathy with them, showed little fear of the soldiers. The Mayor of the city remonstrated with the rioters, but with little result. He called out the fire department, which cleared the streets by turning the hose on the mobs. But this only resulted in diverting the riot from one place in the city to another. Only a rain on Sunday dampened the ardor of the rioters. Order was outwardly restored by Sunday evening, but even thereafter Negroes were killed.

Even though the riot differed from the Russian variety in that it was not instigated and abetted by the government and the military, it brings nothing but shame to this nation. The thoughtful people of Atlanta are of course aroused in condemnation of this outbreak. They feel the humiliation that has befallen their city. Some 300 prominent men assembled in mass meeting to consider the emergency. They denounced the yellow journalism which brought it about, and urged the closing up of the low dives and the putting of a greater restriction upon all saloons. Atlanta is not a typical southern city, and this outbreak ought not to be regarded as typical of the South. Nevertheless

there are other places in the South where a similar anti-Negro riot
might at any time take place. We hope that the governing powers of
Atlanta will first see to it that mob violence is repressed with a strong
hand, and that those who incited it as well as those who led it are
indicted and punished; then that some thorough method of dealing
with Negro crime is adopted. Not only is such a mob as that wicked—
it is futile. In controlling lawless Blacks the appeal to terror has con-
sistently been vain. . . . The Colored population in all parts of the land
has been too much herded, good and bad together. Some way must be
found by which the energies of the Colored people themselves can be
enlisted in the control of the lawless members of the race. It is about
time that Americans learned the folly of attempting government by
murder.

# The Springfield, Illinois Race Riot of 1908*

*James L. Crouthamel*

Springfield, Illinois at the turn of the twentieth century, was one
of those midwestern cities which served as the mercantile center for a
large rural population. Located in the middle of the rich farmland of
central Illinois, it provided this area with an aggressive approach to
business that resembled that of the Yankee. But in its attitude toward
race relations, Springfield was more southern than northern. The fact
that Abraham Lincoln lived most of his adult life here, or that the city
was the state capital of an urban, industrial state, had little effect on
the way in which the residents treated the Negro. In August, 1908,
as the city was preparing to celebrate the centennial of the birth of its
famous son, a violent and bloody race riot struck Springfield.

People who knew Springfield well were not surprised at this outburst
of mob violence. The capital had a reputation, partly justified, of being
one of the most corrupt midwestern cities. Vice was a business protected
by the authorities and overlooked by the respectable citizens. Staid
Jacksonville, thirty-five miles to the west, believed that the capital

* Published by the Association for the Study of Negro Life and History, Inc., in the
July, 1960, *Journal of Negro History*, 164–175, 180–181.

could rival Chicago and San Francisco in the wickedness of its saloons, brothels, and narcotics dens. The *Chicago Daily News* agreed that "Vice and other forms of lawbreaking have been given a wide latitude here. The notoriety of Springfield's evil resorts has been widespread."[1]

Washington Street east of the capital was the center of this vice. Running between the Sangamon County Court House and the county jail, Washington Street was only two blocks north of the capital building and four blocks from Lincoln's home. Here, especially between Ninth and Eleventh Streets, Springfield's "evil resorts" were concentrated—brothels, saloons, gambling dens, secondhand stores, and pawn shops. The Negro residential area flanked these blocks on both sides and extended to the east. Washington Street, the "block of crime," was noted for its lawlessness. Much of the political corruption for which the capital was notorious took place here; Negro votes were bought and sold and the "degenerate" police force was "fixed." Policemen refused to enter this area unarmed or alone. On Christmas Day, 1865, two men were killed here in a clash between policemen and newly-discharged soldiers. Four years later a murder was committed on the same street, and in 1906 another murder. In 1905 a fatal duel was fought on Washington Street, and, in all, twenty-five men had been beaten or killed on this street since the Civil War.[2] This section of the state capital was truly a "disgrace and a stench to the civilized world."[3]

Race relations in Illinois, as throughout the nation, were at a critical point of development at the turn of the century. Feeling against the Negro ran high in Illinois because of the huge Negro influx to urban centers such as Chicago, Peoria, East St. Louis, and Springfield. This threatened the jobs of the Whites as well as their superiority at the ballot box.[4] In "Bloody Williamson" County in Southern Illinois, for example, nonunionized Negro miners acted as strikebreakers, with the result that in 1898 and 1899 violence flared at Virden and Carter-

[1] *Jacksonville* (Illinois) *Daily Journal* (August 18, 1908); *Chicago Daily News*, quoted in Chicago Commission on Race Relations, "The Springfield Riot," *The Negro in Chicago* (Chicago: University of Chicago Press, 1922), p. 71.

[2] (Springfield) *Illinois State Journal* (August 16, 1908).

[3] *Joliet Weekly News* (August 20, 1908).

[4] See Chicago Commission on Race Relations, *The Negro in Chicago*, passim.; Rayford W. Logan, *The Negro in American Life and Thought. The Nadir 1877–1901* (New York: Dial Press, 1954), passim.; John Hope Franklin, *From Slavery to Freedom. A History of American Negroes* (2nd ed.; New York: Alfred A. Knopf, Inc. 1956), pp. 426–435.

ville with seven Negro miners killed. Added to the threat of cheap Negro labor in the depressed mines were traditions of White supremacy dating back to ante-bellum days. Many Illinois towns prohibited Negroes from settling within their city limits, and few Illinois juries would convict a White of killing a Negro.[5]

In the middle of August, 1908, a Negro was in the country jail on Washington Street, indicted by the grand jury for the murder of a White man and awaiting trial. He was Joe James, a young vagrant from Birmingham, Alabama, who had stabbed to death Clergy A. Ballard early on the morning of July 5. Ballard, a middle-aged mining engineer, apparently discovered James in the bedroom of his pretty sixteen-year-old daughter Blanche (trying to "outrage" her, the local newspaper reasoned), struggled with the intruder and was badly cut with a razor. The intruder fled, but Ballard died of his wounds within a few hours. James, who had been released from the city jail only half a day earlier, was arrested and identified by Blanche and her brothers as the intruder. An infuriated mob snatched James from the police and beat him badly before he was taken safely into custody.[6]

After five weeks, it would seem that Springfield's citizenry had forgotten about James. Their attention was centered on more immediate concerns. The price of farm commodities had dropped, but the Springfield Senators were leading the Three I baseball league. Late summer clearance sales were in progress and, most important, the presidential sweepstakes of 1908 had just been launched with the nominations of Republican William Howard Taft and Democrat William Jennings Bryan, who was having a third try at the White House with the slogan "Shall the People Rule?" A bitter Republican primary fight for the gubernatorial nomination had resulted in the selection of incumbent Governor Charles S. Deneen. Also of local interest, the Prohibitionist Party state convention was about to meet at Springfield's St. Nicholas Hotel to nominate state officers. On hand to lead the forces against Demon Rum was their presidential candidate, Eugene Chaffin of Chicago. The Prohibitionists were expected to poll at least 100,000 votes in Illinois in November.[7]

---

[5] Paul M. Augle, *Bloody Williamson: A Chapter in American Lawlessness* (New York: Alfred A. Knopf, Inc., 1952), pp. 98–115.

[6] *Illinois State Journal* (July 5, 6, 1908), 1.

[7] (Springfield) *Illinois State Register* (July–August, 1908), passim.; *Illinois State Journal* (July–August, 1908), passim.; *Jacksonville Daily Journal* (July–August, 1908), passim.

On the morning of August 14, as the capital's residents read their newspapers their thoughts were quickly focused to the Negro question.[8] As they sipped their coffee they saw banner headlines in the *Illinois State Journal* shouting "NEGRO'S HEINOUS CRIME" or in the rival *Illinois State Register* "DRAGGED FROM HER BED AND OUTRAGED BY NEGRO." The night before, the papers stated, a Mrs. Nellie Hallam had been assaulted and raped by a Negro. Quickly, no doubt, their thoughts went back to the events of a month earlier and the fact that Joe James, the Negro murderer, was in the county jail. Two outrages by Negroes in only five weeks!

That same morning George Richardson, a Negro, was arrested as he went to mow a lawn near the Hallam house, and he was identified by Mrs. Hallam as her assailant. Richardson was clapped in the county jail with James, and the story of his crime, as related by Mrs. Hallam and the newspapers, quickly circulated through the city.

Attractive, twenty-one-year-old Nellie Hallam had been married for four years to Earl Hallam, a streetcar conductor who worked until late at night. She was, said the local press, "a quiet, respectable young married woman, who had just four weeks ago buried her only living child." Usually she would retire early and leave a light burning in the bedroom until her husband returned from work. About 11:30 on the night of August 13 Mrs. Hallam was awakened by the touch of someone on her bed. Seeing the light turned down she asked: "Earl, what are you doing?" "I guess I am drunk," a muffled voice replied. Thinking this unusual she cried out, hoping to arouse her husband's parents who lived next door. But she was grasped by the throat and heard a strange voice hiss: "Keep still or I'll kill you." She could see by the dim light that her assailant was a Negro.

The intruder pulled Mrs. Hallam by the throat into the kitchen adjoining the bedroom, then onto the porch, down two steps and across the rough stone sidewalk, and then he fled. She was left bleeding and bruised, half-unconscious and thoroughly frightened in the garden. In a few minutes she was able to scream, rousing her in-laws and most

---

[8] The following account of the riot is taken from: *Illinois State Register, Illinois State Journal, Jacksonville Daily Journal, St. Louis Post-Dispatch, New York Times, New York Tribune, New York American, Chicago Daily Tribune*, August 14–31, 1908; Chicago Commission on Race Relations, *The Negro in Chicago*, pp. 67–71; Adjutant General of Illinois, *Biennial Report, 1907–1908* (Springfield, 1909), pp. 263–270; William E. Walling, "Race War in the North," *The Independent*, LXV (September 3, 1908), 529–534.

of the neighborhood. The assailant's motive had been rape, apparently, because nothing was stolen and he had never mentioned robbery. It was soon discovered that he had gained entry by cutting the back screen door. Mrs. Hallam was sure that she could identify him.

The newspapers printed a gruesome account of the incident which heightened racial tensions. Editorially, the two local papers called for prompt punishment of the perpetrator of this "hellish" outrage and the suppression of the Washington Street establishments that bred "scores of worthless and lawless" Negroes.

The accused George Richardson was, according to the newspaper accounts, an ex-convict in his early thirties who had served time for murder and had been out of prison for only two years. (Actually, Richardson was a sober and industrious citizen who had never been arrested before.) Mrs. Hallam was able to identify him at a preliminary hearing by his voice, not by his appearance, although later she was able to pick him out of a line-up as her attacker. On the basis of Mrs. Hallam's testimony, Richardson was charged with rape and bound over to the grand jury. He had come to the hearing protesting his innocence, and he and his wife swore that they were at home, several blocks from the Hallam house, at the time of the attack. This testimony convinced no one after Mrs. Hallam's positive identification. Later that afternoon small groups of irate citizens began to mill around the jail where the two Negroes, James and Richardson, were being held. The crowd was not yet a mob; it was leaderless and nonviolent, and the sheriff managed to preserve order all afternoon. He made no attempt to disperse the crowd which, by 5:00 P.M. of that hot August Friday, had grown to about 4,000 persons. Many were merely curious bystanders, many were tourists and shoppers in town for the evening and anxious to see what the excitement was about, others were youthful thrill-seekers, but many were motivated by race hatred and, in the case of immigrant laborers, anxious to put the competing Negro in his place.

The sheriff by five o'clock had become very concerned about the safety of his prisoners, his jail, and himself. The size of the crowd was menacing, and in their pushing and joggling they portended violence. By removing the Negro captives, Sheriff Charles Werner reasoned, he could ensure their safety and get the crowd to disperse, since without the prisoners there would be no reason for milling around the jail. So the authorities arranged to divert the attention of the crowd by sending fire engines dashing down the street in front of the prison, while

Richardson and James were taken out the rear into a waiting automobile and rushed to the outlying village of Sherman. Here they were put on a train for Bloomington where they would be safe in the state prison until their trial.

The crowd outside was in an ugly mood. The sun had raised tempers; many of the crowd had missed their dinners, which added to their irritation; and the authorities seemed to be taking no heed of their presence. By sundown the crowd had become an angry mob.

The more aggressive and able men became the mob's leaders, and they set up a shout for the Negro prisoners. Sheriff Werner appeared, awed by the size of the throng before him, and he tried to convince the people that the Negroes were gone, that there was no reason to congregate before the jail. Few persons heard him above the din of the mob, and those that heard did not believe him. Finally he was able to convince those within earshot that they should appoint a delegation to search the jail. Part of the mob conferred and a committee was jostled forward, amid shouts of suspicion and disbelief, to accompany the sheriff into the prison.

The air was tense with expectancy as the mob awaited the return of their representatives. Finally the committee emerged, empty-handed, and reported that Richardson and James were nowhere to be seen. Some believed the Sheriff had been telling the truth, that the captives had been removed. But many felt the officials were lying—the prisoners were merely hidden. It was clear, regardless, that the Negro prisoners were not available to be punished by the mob.

Should no one be punished for the brutal crimes? The story circulated through the gathering at dusk that the owner and driver of the car which had removed the Negroes from their grasp was Harry T. Loper, the owner of a restaurant five blocks from the jail. Perhaps one of the sheriff's deputies told them. Perhaps Sheriff Werner himself wanted to ease the pressure on the jail and himself by diverting the mob elsewhere. With no Negro prisoners to punish, the mob could at least wreak havoc on the person and property of Harry Loper.

At the restaurant they milled about, hooting and threatening, but with no one willing to take the first violent step. Loper appeared in the doorway with a gun, ready to protect his person if not his property. He later explained to the newspapers:

> I have been through one riot, in Cincinatti in '83, the greatest in the country; when one hundred men were killed. It was to avoid

loss of life that I took those men out of town. I did not want to favor the man [Richardson]; I have no interest in him whatever, and would go just as far to punish him as anybody, but after going through the Cincinatti riot, and knowing this Sheriff as I do, I knew he would be killed first before he would let the jail be taken. I thought I would save life by removing the colored men.[9]

Violence started at Loper's about 8:30 P.M. when someone over-turned Loper's automobile standing in front of the restaurant. Then a brick was hurled through the plate-glass window of the building. Policemen and local units of the militia, which had been called out an hour earlier, were helpless to stay the mob. Many of the crowd had spent the waiting hours drinking, and beer bottles were thrown along with the bricks. Each crash brought new cheers and added to the flames of excitement. Cries of "Curse the day that Lincoln freed the nigger" and "niggers must depart from Springfield" came from the mob. Someone shouted: "Abe Lincoln brought them to Springfield and we will drive them out," and again "we want the nigger and we will apply the rope." The policemen could only smile and watch; none were ready to step into the path of the flying missiles, and they were too small a group to stop a mob of thousands. The entire front of the restaurant was quickly demolished.

The rioters were led into the interior of Loper's by a woman, later identified as Kate Howard, a plump, middle-aged widow whom the local press described as "a new Joan of Arc."[10] "What the hell are you fellows afraid of?" she asked. "Come on and I will show you fellows how to do it. Women want protection and this seems to be the only way to get it." Mirrors and furniture, bottles and glasses, were quickly destroyed. Within an hour the restaurant was completely wrecked, a total loss to Loper. What was not destroyed was carried away—the chandeliers, furniture, and fixtures were piled in the street and later burned. The stock of the bar was rapidly consumed, adding to the fever pitch of the mob. Thousands of spectators had gathered by this time, watching the mob and cheering them on with frenzied shouting and curses, the children as excited as their parents.

The "climax of the evening" occurred shortly before ten o'clock. One of the group applied a torch to Loper's automobile and to the piles of loot. Alcohol was added to the blaze and at the same time

---

[9] *Illinois State Journal* (August 15, 1908).

[10] *Ibid.* (August 16, 1908).

policemen finally fired on the mob which had begun to shoot up the remains of the restaurant. Two waiters at Loper's were hit. One, Louis Johnson, was fatally wounded by a stray bullet through his abdomen. Another lost his right arm because of cuts from flying glass.

At this point Mayor Roy R. Reece appeared in the middle of the crowd and made an appeal for law and order. But his reading of the riot act was shouted down and the Mayor was almost crushed by the mass of people. He sought refuge in nearby Mueller's Cigar Store where he spent the remainder of the evening.

Meanwhile, part of the mob had not gone to Loper's but remained at the jail, not convinced that Richardson and James were gone for good. Here they hurled bricks and insults at the police and the militia defending the bastion. Another committee was appointed to search, and they reported to the mob again that the two Negro prisoners had indeed been removed. Hearing this, the throng slowly retreated from the jail, and by 10:00 P.M. this area was almost deserted. Shortly after this time the incendiaries in front of Loper's restaurant had begun to leave. The mob's appetite for violence not having reached satiety, they decided to inflict a general punishment on Springfield's Negro population. By this time, approximately 10:00 P.M., dozens of spectators had been hit by stray bullets and flying glass, and many policemen and militiamen were clubbed or hit.

There had been isolated attacks on innocent Negroes while the mob was at Loper's and the jail. At least five Negro porters were beaten at the railroad depots. Several attacks were made on the Negro residential area about eight o'clock with Negroes seeking refuge in streetcars. But as crowds clogged the streets, the streetcar service had to be abandoned and terrified Blacks were dragged from the cars by frenzied Whites. One such Negro fled to Court House Square, where presidential candidate Engene Chafin was speaking to a Prohibitionist rally. With no place to hide, the Negro darted onto the speaker's platform behind Chafin. "Stand back, gentlemen," the candidate warned the pursuers, "or I'll shoot the first one of you who touches this man." The Negro slipped off into the crowd, and Chafin was stoned by the crowd, his face badly bruised.

The most concerted attack on the Negro residential district was at about eleven o'clock, after Loper's had been wrecked and the rioters had left the jail. Property valued at more than $150,000 was lost, as the mob wrecked almost every building on Washington, Jefferson, and Madison Streets between Eighth and Twelfth Streets. It appears that the mob leaders were careful in destroying only homes and businesses which were either owned by Negroes or served a Negro clientele. (White handkerchiefs marked the homes and businesses of Whites, and these were left untouched in the midst of the general destruction.) Secondhand stores were looted for guns, ammunition, and other weapons. Bars such as "Dandy Jim" Steele's Delmonico Saloon were ransacked and many bottles of liquor carried away. Barrels of whiskey were burned in the streets. From the restaurant of Charley Lee, a Negro, over $200 worth of champagne was carried off, bought in anticipation of the tourist trade which the state fair would bring.

Much of the eastern end of the city was in flames by 1:00 A.M. The first fires started at the corner of Ninth and Jefferson Streets, and they spread quickly along the rows of clapboard wooden structures. A whole row of hovels on both sides of Tenth Street north of Madison burned to the ground, and then the red light district along Ninth Street. In all, eighteen separate fires burned simultaneously, with a four-square-block area between Ninth and Eleventh Streets and Madison and Jefferson Streets leveled by flame. The city firemen were helpless, because the mob would allow them to save only the lumber-yards in the area.

The casualties continued to mount. More stray bullets whizzed through the streets after the looting of guns from the pawn shops and as many in the mob became more intoxicated. Any Negro unlucky enough to be caught by the mob was beaten, including many of the Negro hotel workers in the city, stranded at their jobs when the rioting started. The star pitcher for Springfield's league-leading baseball team was shot in the leg. Hidden in the crowd, many persons delighted in throwing bricks at police and militia. By Monday morning four Whites all of them spectators, would die of wounds from stray bullets. The culmination of this violence was the lynching of two Negroes.

The first victim was Scott Burton, an old, inoffensive Negro barber. About 2:00 A.M. a mob set fire to Burton's wooden frame house, and the old Negro grabbed his shotgun as he fled the blaze. Several shots came from the mob, so Burton fired a load of shot into the mob to defend himself. In turn he was shot four times by the mob, and his fallen body was dragged through the streets on a rope. Finally a likely-looking tree was found and Burton was lynched. Several persons began to mutilate his corpse still further with guns and knives, but at this moment a large enough detachment of militia from Decatur arrived to disperse the crowd and cut down Burton's dead body.

Judge Lynch's second victim was an 84-year-old Negro cobbler named William Donegan, whose good reputation was marred, in the eyes of the rioters, by the fact that he had been married to a White woman for over thirty years. Donegan was found sleeping in his backyard and quickly hanged to a tree across the street, only one block from the State House. Not yet dead, his throat was then cut and his body hacked with knives. Again militia arrived and dispersed the lynchers, and amazingly, the old cobbler was still alive. He was rushed to the hospital, but he died the next morning.

Most of the damage had been done by the time these lynchings occurred. By early Saturday morning the mob was tired and order was restored. The riot was checked, and remained checked, largely because of the intervention of large numbers of state militia. Local units of the militia were called out at six o'clock on Friday evening, but there were not enough of them to control the mobs. Governor Deneen, therefore, at the urging of Sheriff Werner called in by telephone and telegraph militia companies from Peoria, Pekin, Bloomington, Quincy, and Chicago. Enough men had arrived by 3:30 on Saturday morning to be able to take control of many of the trouble spots. By breakfast time about 1,800 militia were camped at the arsenal, the capital grounds, and Lincoln Park. The total by Sunday stood at 3,691 men commanded by Major General Edward C. Young.

Springfield resembled a city in wartime on the morning after the riot, with squads of soldiers patroling the streets, and entire batallions concentrated in the Negro area. Tents were pitched on the grounds of the state buildings and cavalry units rode through the downtown area. These soldiers did their job well—the city remained relatively quiet for the remainder of the weekend. "Cowed by the display of military force," said a local newspaper, "and awed by superior armament and grim determination by the authorities, the spirit of the mob was broken at the first clash and the rioters fell back, beaten yet breathing threat of violence."

A large-scale exodus of Springfield's terrified Negro population was one of the first concrete results of the riot. About 3,000 Negroes sought refuge at the National Guard's Camp Lincoln on the outskirts of the city. Few Negroes were foolish enough to report for work on Saturday, and most of those that did were sent home by their employers. Many firms discharged their Negro help, and others received anonymous threats to do so or else suffer the consequences. Since many Negroes were now jobless as well as homeless, small wonder that thousands of them left the city and never returned. Hundreds left on foot while the more fortunate rode in extra coaches which the Wabash Railroad put on to carry the refugees to points west. (But a few Illinois towns—Jacksonville and Peoria, for example—refused to allow these Negroes within their city limits.) Some sought asylum in Chicago and St. Louis. This exodus caused another casualty, the seventh death to result from the riot. A Negro baby died of exposure near Pittsfield, Illinois, as her parents were walking west to escape the mob.

Springfield's citizens encouraged this Negro migration. Few Negroes got their jobs back, and grocers refused to sell food to the Blacks. (The state of Illinois was forced to buy $10,000 worth of groceries for the capital's Negroes.) The press agreed that the city would be better off with fewer Negroes, and surrounding towns took precautions so that they would not pick up the emigrants. At the village of Buffalo, fifteen miles from Springfield, this sign was posted at the railway station:

All niggers are warned out of town by Monday, 12 M. sharp.
— BUFFALO SHARP SHOOTERS

One experienced reporter felt that these racial tensions in Springfield would last in spite of the exodus. William E. Walling, writing in *The Independent*, believed "the whole awful and menacing truth" was "that a large part of the White population of Lincoln's home, supported largely by the farmers and miners of the neighboring towns, have initiated a permanent warfare with the Negro race."

.    .    .    .    .    .    .    .    .

The race war at Springfield, especially at so untimely a moment as the preparations for the Lincoln centennial celebration, stirred both Negroes and certain northern Whites out of their lethargy and demonstrated the need for a more powerful protest organization. Reporter William E. Walling, who covered the riot for the liberal weekly *The Independent*, was shocked by the events at the capital and issued a plea for a revival of the spirit of abolitionism to protect the Negro and safeguard his rights. Several northeastern reformers had read Walling's concluding plea, and on the basis of this they issued a call for a conference to meet at Springfield, Illinois, the scene of the riot, on February 12, 1909, the Lincoln centennial, to discuss the Negro problem. The call was written by Oswald Garrison Villard and linked the old abolitionist spirit to the new protest movement. The leaders were two New York social workers, Mary White Ovington and Henry

Moskovitz, and among those attending the conference with them were Walling, Villard, DuBois, John Dewey, James Adams, William Dean Howells, John Milholland, and Livingston Farrand—a very distinguished gathering of social workers, educators, jurists, professors, religious leaders, and publicists. The Conference, meeting only six months after the riot, established the National Association for the Advancement of Colored People, incorporated in 1910.

Out of the violence at Springfield had come the organization of the first really effective Negro protest. The NAACP was not able to prevent the recurrence of race violence—witness the rash of race riots immediately after World War I—but it could focus national attention on these incidents, point the finger of scorn, and bring Negro discontent into the open. Each case of discrimination was publicized and many cases were brought into the appeal court systems with NAACP financial aid. Had the Springfield race riot not occurred at such an inopportune moment and at a place where the Lincoln aura was the strongest, the NAACP might not have been established.

# Chapter Two

# World War I:
# The Effect of Job Competition

In the first two decades of the twentieth century there was a vast out-
pouring of Negroes from the South in search of jobs in the major industrial
centers of the North and Midwest. The demand for a large labor force in the
cities was compounded by the outbreak of war in Europe in 1914. Eager to
attract cheap labor to swell the numbers needed to fill the war orders from
European countries, industrialists distributed leaflets and sent agents into the
South in an effort to entice persons to the North. The desire to travel North—
to the Promised Land—was intensified by the deprivation created by poor farming conditions. The hope of economic improvement, of steady work, of release
from an oppressive social system brought millions into the cities. Indeed, the
great migration of Negroes into the small and large urban centers is one of
the most important facts of contemporary America.

The dream of betterment, however, was frequently punctured by lower- and
middle-class Whites. War periods are generally characterized by unrest and
insecurity, which result from the disruption of traditional life patterns. In times
of national distress, minority groups are made to bear the brunt of individual
and general discontent. The closer contact generated by mobility into and
within the city in the period from 1914 to 1919 further heightened tensions

between newly arrived Blacks and the older residents of the cities, tensions which resulted in three major riots: East St. Louis in 1917; Washington, D.C. and Chicago in 1919.

Although the causes of these riots were complex, the two major interlacing factors that produced hostilities within the Caucasion communities were fears of job competition and of sexual assault. In the first major riot in East St. Louis, there were actually two serious clashes within one month. The first outbreak occurred soon after a meeting in which the president of a trade union led a delegation before the Mayor in order to protest the emigration of southern Negroes. The delegation insisted that Negroes had been invited to the city because of the lack of White men for women in the community. Also underlying this indictment was the fear of the increasing numbers of laborers. Adding fuel to the situation was a rumor that a Negro had killed a White man—and a riot ensued. The militia quickly quelled the disturbance. But a little more than a month later, an automobile sped into the Negro quarter and its occupants opened fire indiscriminately into homes. Fear gripped the Negroes who armed themselves. When a second car appeared, an unmarked police vehicle, Negroes fired into it and killed two policemen. The incident unleashed the second riot. At the conclusion of the violence, approximately 10,000 Negroes made their exodus from the "Black Valley" ghetto of East St. Louis.

Three other riots occurred in 1917, one of them in Houston, Texas involving Negro soldiers. Northern Negro soldiers, unaccustomed to Jim Crow laws, vigorously protested segregation and discrimination practices. The rising tension between the races climaxed when a White policeman beat and jailed two Negro military police officers. Rumors that the men had been killed spread through the army camp, touching off the fracas which involved hundreds of military men.

The post–World War I period too was one of extreme anxiety throughout the country. Large-scale unemployment, the numbers of encamped servicemen awaiting discharge, dislocation of individuals and families, frenzied reactions to alleged radical political movements, and other factors turned cities like Washington, D.C. and Chicago into human tinderboxes. At the termination of the war, Negroes found themselves victimized by reports that "French-women-ruined-Negroes" were returning to the country from France to destroy the supremacy of White men.

Washington, D.C., in the summer of 1919, was a city caught in the throes of sudden, energetic adjustment. Basically a southern city, Washington had been inundated by thousands of Negroes seeking employment. Returning White servicemen resented the migration and the "independent" attitude of the previously subservient Negroes. The situation was accurately described by an Interracial Commission many years later:

A week after the Armistice one might have observed a subtle but ominous change. Distrust was awakened. What would be the attitude of Negro troops when they returned from France? Rumors filled the air, and by the time the soldiers began to return suspicion and fear had taken deep hold upon both races. Mob violence, which had greatly declined during the war, burst out afresh. In city after city race riots flamed up, with casualties on both sides. The tension tightened everywhere, and with dread suspicion, the nation awaited the outcome.*

In mid-July, newspapers carried stories of six attacks by Negroes on White women. After one report, gangs of sailors, soldiers, and marines, many awaiting discharge from the services, began halting streetcars and beating up Negroes. The riot was under way.

In contrast with many other outbreaks of violence over racial friction, the Chicago riot was not preceded by the excitement over reports of attacks on women or any other crime alleged to have been committed by Negroes. The problem was one of the close proximity of the two races. Between 1910 and 1920, the non-White population of Chicago had increased from 44,000 to 109,000. Chicago was one of the northern cities most heavily affected by the migration of Negroes from the South and was regarded as the "top of the world" to many eager former sharecroppers. Large numbers of Whites had also migrated into the city to work in the industries. Competition in the static housing market and in the diminishing job market brought the two groups into conflict. The predilection of Negroes to vote Republican also stirred feelings of resentment. The Democratic machine was distressed by the election of a Republican city administration and the machine's adherents reflected the sharpness of the discontent by vilifying Negroes. As Negroes moved into Caucasian districts, bombs were thrown and tension heightened. In the midst of a heat wave, a Negro youth accidentally swam across an imaginary segregation line in Lake Michigan. The explosion of violence which followed led to thirty-eight reported deaths; of these twenty-three were Negroes. In all there were 557 injured persons; more than 1,000 buildings burned; and 3,000 Negroes rendered homeless.

A change occurred during the riots of this period. Unlike the relatively passive response of the Negroes in the riots of 1906-1908, there was a determination by Negroes to defend themselves and to retaliate against the attacks of Caucasian mobs. This was particularly evident in the riots of Washington D.C. and Chicago when Negroes formed groups and struck back. Nevertheless, the bulk of damage was in the Negro community, a constant fact in the history of race riots.

---

* "The Interracial Commission Comes of Age," (leaflet; February, 1942).

# East St. Louis (1917)*

It is not without a certain irony that, at the very moment when this country is entering the war to "make the world safe for democracy," a race riot of unexampled brutality should take place in East St. Louis, Illinois. On the two days preceding July 4, the Negroes of that city were anything but "safe." There had been trouble last May, but it was insignificant as compared with the July riots. Forty or fifty of the Colored people were killed; nearly a hundred were taken to hospitals; more than three hundred houses in the Negro quarter were burned to the ground. Thousands of militiamen were summoned to the scene and at last succeeded in quieting the tumult. But the terrible scenes enacted are felt to have disgraced not only the State but the entire country. "One of the worst blots on the good name of an American community in our whole history," is what the *Chicago Tribune* calls the riots. At a meeting held in Carnegie Hall, New York City, in honor of the Russian Commission, ex-President Roosevelt spoke in vehement protest against the "appalling outbreak of savagery," and said, apropos of the new Russia: "Before we speak of justice for others, it behooves us to do justice within our own household." Mr. [Samuel] Gompers, in commenting on the riots, at the same meeting, emphasized the "luring of Negroes" from the South to undermine the working conditions of White men in the North. "The luring of these Colored men to East St. Louis," he declared, "is on a par with the behavior of the brutal, reactionary and tyrannous forces that existed in Old Russia." Mr. Roosevelt took the floor again and retorted: "How can we praise the people of Russia for doing justice to the men within their boundaries if we in any way apologize for murder committed on the helpless? In the past I have listened to the same form of excuse advanced in behalf of the Russian autocracy for pogroms of Jews. Not for a moment shall I acquiesce in any apology for the murder of women and children in our own country."

## How East St. Louis Was Turned Into a Shambles

No two writers agree entirely in their accounts of the beginning of the massacre. Henry M. Hyde, a correspondent of the *Chicago Tribune*, says that on the evening of Sunday, July 1, a Ford automobile,

* From "The Illinois Race War and its Brutal Aftermath," *Current Opinion* (August, 1917), 75–77.

occupied by four men, was driven rapidly through the Negro districts of the city. The four men yelled, cursed and fired revolvers right and left. Some of the shots are said to have entered adjacent buildings, one of them a church, whose bell was rung later. At the ringing of the bell—evidently a preconcerted signal—two hundred armed Negroes assembled and, marching two abreast, started downtown. They were met by a police automobile, also a Ford car and also containing four men, who proved to be police officers in plain clothes. The officers started to explain, but the Negroes refused to listen, and when the car turned fired a volley at the fleeing officers. One of them was instantly killed, another died later. Then hell broke loose. For the greater part of thirty-six hours, Negroes were hunted through the streets like wild animals. A black skin became a death warrant. Man after man, with hands upraised, pleading for his life, was surrounded by groups of men who had never seen him before and who knew nothing about him except that he was Black, and stoned to death. A Negro girl, seeking safety from a band of White men, was attacked by White women, and despite her pleas for mercy had her face smashed by a club wielded by one of the White women. An aged Negro, tottering from a weakness, was seized and hanged to a pole. Three million dollars' worth of property was destroyed. State guardsmen were called out but did nothing. The police seemed helpless or acquiescent. A number of arrests were made, but hardly any one was held. "I have heard of St. Bartholomew's Night," writes Carlos F. Hurd, in the *St. Louis Post-Dispatch*, "I have heard stories of the latter-day crimes of the Turks in Armenia, and I have learned to loath the German army for its barbarity in Belgium. But I do not believe that Moslem fanaticism or Prussian frightfulness could perpetrate murders of more deliberate brutality than those which I saw committed, in daylight, by citizens of the State of Abraham Lincoln."

## Invasion of Negro Labor as a Cause of the Rioting

The cause of the riot in East St. Louis is found by most commentators in the sudden influx of Negroes from the South and in the economic rivalries engendered. Race hatred has doubtless played its part, but the "scab" Negro, coming north to take the place of a White laborer on strike, is held to have been the chief factor in recent disturbances. The low immigration from Europe since the beginning of the war has helped to create an abnormal situation. East St. Louis is a great railroad and manufacturing center, with coal mines near at hand.

Employers have been glad to avail themselves of Negro labor. Ray Stannard Baker writes in *The World's Work* of this shifting of Negro labor:

> The earlier manifestations of the movement were more or less sporadic, due largely to the activities of northern labor agents, especially those representing railroad companies. Trains were backed into several southern cities and hundreds of Negroes were gathered up in a day, loaded into the cars, and whirled away to the North. I was told of instances in which Negro teamsters left their horses standing in the streets, or deserted their jobs and went to the trains without notifying their employers or even going home. But this spring the movement has become more or less organized, and, while not so spectacular, is probably more widespread.

Mr. Baker tells us further that great manufacturing and railroad corporations in the North have regular agents to direct the importations of Negro laborers, and that members of the Negro colonies already established in Pennsylvania, New York and southern New England, are drawing strongly from their compatriots in the South. In certain parts of Georgia and Alabama, especially where the larger tenant farming is still practiced, whole neighborhoods have been depleted of Black men of the best working ages, and often entire families have moved. Between 75,000 and 100,000 have settled in Pennsylvania alone, a large number being employed by the Pennsylvania and Erie Railroads, and still larger numbers by the steel mills, the munition plants and other manufacturing establishments. Mr. Baker calculates that, in all, 400,000 Negroes have gone north during the last eighteen months.

### Plans for Preventing Race Riots in the Future

Federal, state and municipal investigations have all been undertaken to determine where the responsibility for the recent outbreak in East St. Louis belongs. Senator Sherman, in urging the necessity of congressional action, has declared his conviction that "there is as much influence in securing acquittal of guilty men in Illinois as there ever was in Georgia." The Senator stated on the floor of the Senate that the part played by liquor in the course of the trouble had made him from henceforth a "bone-dry Prohibitionist." The *New York Sun* indicts the East St. Louis city administration, and recalls the fact that its own officials have openly admitted that the law is not enforced.

Other papers urge the necessity of establishing in Illinois a state constabulary of the kind now existing in Pennsylvania. But these and similar suggestions deal with symptoms rather than causes. Many of the southern papers take the view that the only real solution of present difficulties is for the Negroes to return to the South. There is a widespread disposition in the South to offer Negroes inducements to return. The *Nashville Tennessean* acknowledges a moral obligation to "protect and care for a race which we alone seem to understand"; and the *Jacksonville Times-Union* remarks:

> The Negroes of the South may see in this East St. Louis affair just what will happen all over the North when there is no longer enough work for all and White men want their jobs. Where are they safest—in a section where a certain offense insures their summary death and good behavior assures them safety, or in a section that in time of passion gives them no assurance of safety at all, and where their color will mark them for assault?

The *Galveston Daily News* is convinced that the true and fundamental solution of this grave problem lies as a matter of duty and policy with the South. It says:

> The South is the Negro's natural habitat, and the South has an economic need of him. The interests of the South and of the Negro are complementary in the truest sense. A policy of justice is likewise the policy of expedience. The Negro labor, which the South indispensably needs for its own economic well-being, can be retained if the South will, in its treatment of the Negro, conform its practices to the chivalrous precepts with which it decorates itself. When the Negro goes north, he is moved more by the repulsion of the conditions that beset him in the South than by the attraction of those that invite him to the North. His natural preference is to live in the South, but that preference is not so strong that it cannot be nullified by the injustices which are done him too frequently in the South. The Negroes of the South are not seeking social equality. They do, however, crave a larger opportunity for educational, economic and social progress than they enjoy, and it is the denial of this which makes so many of them yield to the lure of the North. The South has only to reform its own habits of conduct toward the Negro to keep him contented, and, by doing that, preclude a repetition of the exhibition of savagery which the country has been called on to witness at East St. Louis.

# The Riot of Washington, D. C. (1919)*

Between June 25 and July 7 four or five attempts to commit rape, one of them successful, occurred in an outlying quarter of the city. Descriptions of the assailant in the several cases convinced high police officials that only one Negro was responsible for these crimes. Following July 7 a few other instances were reported, some of which proved groundless, others were merely cases where women were jostled by Negroes; but the public, not weighing the evidence, came pretty generally to believe that an epidemic of crimes against White women was abroad. The wife of a soldier returning from her work shortly after ten o'clock, July 18, was jostled by two Negroes, but within call of several White men. The case furnished the immediate cause of the first riot, which occurred in the southwest section of the city on the following (Saturday) night. A mob of 400 or 500, led by soldiers who sought to avenge what they held to be an attempted assault on the wife of a brother soldier, were dispersed by the police and provost guard after beating two Negroes, one of whom was fifty-five years old. Early Sunday morning a policeman in the southwest section was shot and badly wounded by a Negro whom he had challenged. Between ten o'clock and midnight Sunday night groups of soldiers, sailors, and civilians (none of these groups formidable) pursued and attacked individual Negroes on Pennsylvania Avenue between Seventh Street and the Treasury, carrying their operations to the north front of the latter, and even as far as the White House. Innocent Negroes going home from their work were dragged from streetcars and brutally beaten.

Failure of the police to check the rioters promptly, and in certain instances an attitude on their part of seeming indifference, filled the mob with contempt of authority and set the stage for the demonstration of the following night. In behalf of the police, it may be said that their number—about 840 to a population estimated by the census authorities a year ago as at 401,000—has long been complained of as wholly inadequate. Fully a third of the force, moreover, are new men, chiefly discharged soldiers and unfamiliar with their new duties.

In the early hours of Monday morning the attacks on Negroes were carried into sections where the Black population is heavy. The whole Negro element of Washington became suddenly aware of a war on

---

* "Racial Tension and Race Riots," *The Outlook* (August 6, 1919), 533.

their race, which spared no man of color and stopped not to determine whether or not he belonged to the large class of industrious and orderly Negroes in the city. Always more or less suspicious of the White police, who in Washington outnumber the Negro police about twenty-seven to one, and believing that a Negro on arrest is treated more harshly than a White man, by Monday night the Colored population held themselves to be without police protection. The mob element among the Blacks then armed for war, while many of the better element of their race armed in obedience to the first law of nature.

That night, the determined efforts of the police, aided by cavalry, infantry, marines, and citizens, were powerless to quell the mobs that surged through the principal business streets and in the Black districts. The result was that two Whites, one of them a policeman, and two Blacks were killed, and hundreds, instead of scores, as on the previous evening, wounded. Subsequent deaths as the result of the riots and their aftermath have brought the number of fatalities up to seven.

On Tuesday evening and throughout the remainder of the week, except for the presence of military patrols, the streets of Washington have presented an air of unusual quiet.

The mobs that broke the long record of good order in the national capital—for since 1857, when the Know-Nothing party imported a band of thugs from Baltimore to stage an election riot, there has been no demonstration of factions worthy to be called a riot—were made up almost wholly of boys between eighteen and twenty-five years of age. In part these were composed of young roughs of the city. The rest were soldiers and sailors, either discharged or from nearby camps, and from their appearance doubtless of the hoodlum element of their home towns. The hours they enjoyed in the lust of man-hunting may make these latter especially dangerous in returning to their homes and communicating to their companions the mob spirit. No less dangerous, however, to law and order in this country is the existence of a considerable class in the population, in Washington as well as elsewhere, who, while taking no active part in mob violence, still hold to the belief that only an indiscriminate war on the Negroes can check the individuals who from time to time attempt crimes on White women. How futile the weapon is, however, is seen by the fact that on the third night of the rioting in Washington, still another attempt to assault a White woman was reported just outside the district line in Maryland.

Before this country entered the Great War the Washington police were better acquainted than they are at present with the Negroes of that city and in the main regarded them as law-abiding. Of late, with the great influx of a new and temporary population, generally White, have come many Negroes, and of this number some of vicious character from the states farther south. High wages paid Negro labor during and since the war have, moreover, tended to increase such ill feeling as already existed in certain classes of the Whites against the Negroes, in that the less thrifty of the latter have made poor use of their opportunity—stopping work as soon as they had their week's unusual wages—and some others in their prosperity have become too assertive. This is an indictment to which the great body of Negroes in Washington should not be subjected. The long record of peaceful relations between Whites and Blacks in the city, where each race is dependent upon the other to an extent unknown to the majority of American cities, should for the good of all concerned be resumed at once. Indeed, on the day after each night's disorder there was no indication on the streets or in places of business that the usual relations between the two races had been at all affected. The leaders of the Colored people in Washington have in the past month again and again offered their aid to assist the authorities in apprehending Negro offenders.

# The Chicago Riot (1919)*

## Background

In July, 1919, a race riot involving Whites and Negroes occurred in Chicago. For some time thoughtful citizens, White and Negro, had sensed increasing tension, but, having no local precedent of riot and wholesale bloodshed, had neither prepared themselves for it nor taken steps to prevent it. The collecting of arms by members of both races was known to the authorities, and it was evident that this was in preparation for aggression as well as for self-defense.

Several minor clashes preceded the riot. On July 3, 1917, a White saloonkeeper who, according to the coroner's physician, died of heart trouble, was incorrectly reported in the press to have been killed by a

---

* Reprinted from *The Negro in Chicago* by the Chicago Commission on Race Relations by permission of The University of Chicago Press. Copyright 1922 by The University of Chicago. All rights reserved. Published September, 1922.

Negro. That evening a party of young White men riding in an automobile fired upon a group of Negroes at Fifty-third and Federal Streets. In July and August of the same year recruits from the Great Lakes Naval Training Station clashed frequently with Negroes, each side accusing the other of being the aggressor.

Gangs of White "toughs," made up largely of the membership of so-called athletic clubs from the neighborhood between Roosevelt Road and Sixty-third Street, Wentworth Avenue and the city limits—a district contiguous to the neighborhood of the largest Negro settlement—were a constant menace to Negroes who traversed sections of the territory going to and returning from work. The activities of these gangs and "athletic clubs" became bolder in the spring of 1919, and on the night of June 21, five weeks before the riot, two wanton murders of Negroes occurred, those of Sanford Harris and Joseph Robinson. Harris returning to his home on Dearborn Street, about 11:30 at night, passed a group of young White men. They threatened him and he ran. He had gone but a short distance when one of the group shot him. He died soon afterward. Policemen who came on the scene made no arrests, even when the assailant was pointed out by a White woman witness of the murder. On the same evening Robinson, a Negro laborer, forty-seven years of age, was attacked while returning from work by a gang of White "roughs" at Fifty-fifth Street and Princeton Avenue, apparently without provocation, and stabbed to death.

Negroes were greatly incensed over these murders, but their leaders, joined by many friendly Whites, tried to allay their fears and counseled patience.

After the killing of Harris and Robinson notices were conspicuously posted on the South Side that an effort would be made to "get all the niggers on July Fourth." The notices called for help from sympathizers. Negroes in turn whispered around the warning to prepare for a riot; and they did prepare.

Since the riot in East St. Louis, July 4, 1917, there had been others in different parts of the country which evidenced a widespread lack of restraint in mutual antipathies and suggested further resorts to lawlessness. Riots and race clashes occurred in Chester, Pennsylvania; Longview, Texas; Coatesville, Pennsylvania; Washington, D.C.; and Norfolk, Virginia, before the Chicago riot.

Aside from general lawlessness and disastrous riots that preceded the riot here discussed, there were other factors which may be mentioned briefly here. In Chicago considerable unrest had been occasioned in industry by increasing competition between White and Negro laborers following a sudden increase in the Negro population due to the migration of Negroes from the South. This increase developed a housing crisis. The Negroes overran the hitherto recognized area of Negro residence. and when they took houses in adjoining neighborhoods friction ensued. In the two years just preceding the riot, twenty-seven Negro dwellings were wrecked by bombs thrown by unidentified persons.

## Story of the Riot

Sunday afternoon, July 27, 1919, hundreds of White and Negro bathers crowded the lakefront beaches at Twenty-sixth and Twenty-ninth Streets. This is the eastern boundary of the thickest Negro residence area. At Twenty-sixth Street Negroes were in great majority; at Twenty-ninth Street there were more Whites. An imaginary line in the water separating the two beaches had been generally observed by the two races. Under the prevailing relations, aided by wild rumors and reports, this line served virtually as a challenge to either side to cross it. Four Negroes who attempted to enter the water from the "White" side were driven away by the Whites. They returned with more Negroes, and there followed a series of attacks with stones, first one side gaining the advantage, then the other.

Eugene Williams, a Negro boy of seventeen, entered the water from the side used by Negroes and drifted across the line supported by a railroad tie. He was observed by the crowd on the beach and promptly became a target for stones. He suddenly released the tie, went down and was drowned. Guilt was immediately placed on Stauber, a young White man, by Negro witnesses who declared that he threw the fatal stone.[1]

White and Negro men dived for the boy without result. Negroes demanded that the policeman present arrest Stauber. He refused; and at this crucial moment arrested a Negro on a White man's complaint. Negroes then attacked the officer. These two facts, the drowning and the refusal of the policeman to arrest Stauber, together marked the beginning of the riot.

Two hours after the drowning, a Negro, James Crawford, fired into a group of officers summoned by the policeman at the beach and was killed by a Negro policeman. Reports and rumors circulated

---

[1] The coroner's jury found that Williams had drowned from fear of stone-throwing which kept him from the shore.

rapidly, and new crowds began to gather. Five White men were injured in clashes near the beach. As darkness came Negroes in White districts to the west suffered severely. Between 9:00 P.M. and 3:00 A.M. twenty-seven Negroes were beaten, seven stabbed, and four shot. Monday morning was quiet, and Negroes went to work as usual.

Returning from work in the afternoon many Negroes were attacked by White ruffians. Streetcar routes, especially at transfer points, were the centers of lawlessness. Trolleys were pulled from the wires, and Negro passengers were dragged into the street, beaten, stabbed, and shot. The police were powerless to cope with these numerous assaults. During Monday, four Negro men and one White assailant were killed, and thirty Negroes were severely beaten in streetcar clashes. Four White men were killed, six stabbed, five shot, and nine severely beaten. It was rumored that the White occupants of the Angelus Building at Thirty-fifth Street and Wabash Avenue had shot a Negro. Negroes gathered about the building. The White tenants sought police protection, and one hundred policemen, mounted and on foot, responded. In a clash with the mob the police killed four Negroes and injured many.

Raids into the Negro residence area then began. Automobiles sped through the streets, the occupants shooting at random. Negroes retaliated by "sniping" from ambush. At midnight surface and elevated car service was discontinued because of a strike for wage increases, and thousands of employees were cut off from work.

On Tuesday, July 29, Negro men en route on foot to their jobs through hostile territory were killed. White soldiers and sailors in uniform, aided by civilians, raided the "Loop" business section, killing two Negroes and beating and robbing several others. Negroes living among White neighbors in Englewood, far to the south, were driven from their homes, their household goods were stolen, and their houses were burned or wrecked. On the West Side an Italian mob, excited by a false rumor that an Italian girl had been shot by a Negro, killed Joseph Lovings, a Negro.

Wednesday night at 10:30 Mayor Thompson yielded to pressure and asked the help of the three regiments of militia which had been stationed in nearby armories during the most severe rioting, awaiting the call. They immediately took up positions throughout the South Side. A rainfall Wednesday night and Thursday kept many people in their homes, and by Friday the rioting had abated. On Saturday incendiary fires burned forty-nine houses in the immigrant neighborhood west of the Stockyards. Nine hundred and forty-eight people, mostly Lithuanians, were made homeless, and the property loss was about $250,000. Responsibility for the fires was never fixed.

The total casualties of this reign of terror were thirty-eight deaths— fifteen white, twenty-three Negro—and 537 people injured. Forty-one per cent of the reported clashes occurred in the white neighborhood near the Stockyards between the south branch of the Chicago River and Fifty-fifth Street, Wentworth Avenue and the city limits, and 34 per cent in the "Black Belt" between Twenty-second and Thirty-ninth Streets, Wentworth Avenue and Lake Michigan. Others were scattered.

Responsibility for many attacks was definitely placed by many witnesses upon the "athletic clubs," including Ragen's Colts, the Hamburgers, Aylwards, Our Flag, the Standard, the Sparklers, and several others. The mobs were made up for the most part of boys between fifteen and twenty-two. Older persons participated, but the youth of the rioters was conspicuous in every clash. Little children witnessed the brutalities and frequently pointed out the injured when the police arrived.

### Rumors and the Riot

Wild rumors were in circulation by word of mouth and in the press throughout the riot and provoked many clashes. These included stories of atrocities committed by one race against the other. Reports of the numbers of white and Negro dead tended to produce a feeling that the score must be kept even. Newspaper reports, for example, showed 6 per cent more whites injured than Negroes. As a matter of fact there were 28 per cent more Negroes injured than whites. The *Chicago Tribune* on July 29 reported twenty persons killed, of whom thirteen were White and seven Colored. The true figures were exactly the opposite.

Among the rumors provoking fear were numerous references to the arming of Negroes. In the *Daily News* of July 30, for example, appeared the subheadline: "ALDERMAN JOS. Mc DONOUGH TELLS HOW HE WAS SHOT AT ON SOUTH SIDE VISIT. SAYS ENOUGH AMMUNITION IN SECTION TO LAST FOR YEARS OF GUERRILLA WARFARE." In the article following, the reference to ammunition was repeated but not elaborated or explained.

The Alderman was quoted as saying that the Mayor contemplated opening up Thirty-fifth and Forty-seventh Streets in order that Colored people might get to their work. He thought this would be most unwise for, he stated, "They are armed and White people are not. We must defend ourselves if the city authorities won't protect us." Continuing his story, he described bombs going off: "I saw White men and women running through the streets dragging children by the hands and carrying babies in their arms. Frightened White men told me the police captains had just rushed through the district crying, 'For God's sake, arm; they are coming; we cannot hold them.' "

Whether or not the Alderman was correctly quoted, the effect of such statements on the public was the same. There is no record in any of the riot testimony in the coroner's office or state's attorney's office of any bombs going off during the riot, nor of police captains warning the White people to arm, nor of any fear by Whites of a Negro invasion. In the Berger Odman case before a coroner's jury there was a statement to the effect that a sergeant of police warned the Negroes of Ogden Park to arm and to shoot at the feet of rioters if they attempted to invade the few blocks marked off for Negroes by the police. Negroes were warned, not Whites.

## Conduct of the Police

Chief of Police John J. Garrity, in explaining the inability of the police to curb the rioters, said that there was not a sufficient force to police one-third of the city. Aside from this, Negroes distrusted the White police officers, and it was implied by the Chief and stated by State's Attorney Hoyne, that many of the police were "grossly unfair in making arrests." There were instances of actual police participation in the rioting as well as neglect of duty. Of 229 persons arrested and accused of various criminal activities during the riot, 154 were Negroes and 75 were Whites. Of those indicted, 81 were Negroes and 47 were Whites. Although this, on its face, would indicate great riot activity on the part of Negroes, further reports of clashes show that of 520 persons injured, 342 were Negroes and 178 were Whites. The fact that twice as many Negroes appeared as defendants and twice as many Negroes as Whites were injured, leads to the conclusion that Whites were not apprehended as readily as Negroes.

Many depredations outside the "Black Belt" were encouraged by the absence of policemen. Out of a force of 3,000 police, 2,800 were massed in the "Black Belt" during the height of the rioting. In the "Loop" district, where two Negroes were killed and several others wounded, there were only three policemen and one sergeant. The

Stockyards district, where the greatest number of injuries occurred, was also weakly protected.

## The Militia

Although Governor Lowden had ordered the militia into the city promptly and they were on hand on the second day of the rioting, their services were not requested by the Mayor and Chief of Police until the evening of the fourth day. The reason expressed by the chief for this delay was a belief that inexperienced militiamen would add to the deaths and disorder. But the troops, when called, proved to be clearly of high character, and their discipline was good, not a case of breach of discipline being reported during their occupation. They were distributed more proportionately through all the riotous areas than the police and, although they reported some hostility from members of "athletic clubs," the rioting soon ceased.

## Restoration of Order

Throughout the rioting various social organizations and many citizens were at work trying to hold hostilities in check and to restore order. The Chicago Urban League, Wabash Avenue Y.M.C.A., American Red Cross, and various other social organizations and the churches of the Negro community gave attention to caring for stranded Negroes, advising them of dangers, keeping them off the streets and, in such ways as were possible, cooperating with the police. The packing companies took their pay to Negro employees, and various banks made loans. Local newspapers in their editorial columns insistently condemned the disorder and counseled calmness.

.    .    .    .    .    .    .    .    .    .

This study of the facts of the riot of 1919, the events as they happened hour by hour, the neighborhoods involved, the movements of mobs, the part played by rumors, and the handling of the emergency by the various authorities, shows certain outstanding features which may be listed as follows:

1) The riot violence was not continuous hour by hour, but was intermittent.

2) The greatest number of injuries occurred in the district west and inclusive of Wentworth Avenue, and south of the south branch of the Chicago River to Fifty-fifth Street, or in the Stockyards district. The next greatest number occurred in the so-called Black Belt: Twenty-second to Thirty-ninth streets,

inclusive, and Wentworth Avenue to the lake, exclusive of Wentworth Avenue; Thirty-ninth to Fifty-fifth Streets, inclusive, and Clark Street to Michigan Avenue, exclusive of Michigan Avenue.

3) Organized raids occurred only after a period of sporadic clashes and spontaneous mob outbreaks.

4) Main thoroughfares witnessed 76 per cent of the injuries on the South Side. The streets which suffered most severely were State, Halsted, Thirty-first, Thirty-fifth, and Forty-seventh. Transfer corners were always centers of disturbances.

5) Most of the rioting occurred after work hours among idle crowds on the streets. This was particularly true after the streetcar strike began.

6) Gangs, particularly of young Whites, formed definite nuclei for crowd and mob formation. "Athletic clubs" supplied the leaders of many gangs.

7) Crowds and mobs engaged in rioting were generally composed of a small nucleus of leaders and an acquiescing mass of spectators. The leaders were mostly young men, usually between the ages of sixteen and twenty-one. Dispersal was most effectively accomplished by sudden, unexpected gun fire.

8) Rumor kept the crowds in an excited, potential mob state. The press was responsible for giving wide dissemination to much of the inflammatory matter in spoken rumors, though editorials calculated to allay race hatred and help the forces of order were factors in the restoration of peace.

9) The police lacked sufficient forces for handling the riot; they were hampered by the Negroes' distrust of them; routing orders and records were not handled with proper care; certain officers were undoubtedly unsuited to police or riot duty.

10) The militiamen employed in this riot were of an unusually high type. This unquestionably accounts for the confidence placed in them by both races. Riot training, definite orders, and good staff work contributed to their efficiency.

11) There was a lack of energetic cooperation between the police department and the state's attorney's office in the discovery and conviction of rioters. The riot was merely a symptom of serious and profound disorders lying beneath the surface of race relations in Chicago.

# Chapter Three

# World War II: The Internal Race War

In the interim period from 1919 to 1935, there were sporadic outbursts of race riots and many lynchings in rural areas of the South and Southwest. Riots took place in Lexington, Kentucky; Ocoee, Florida; Tulsa, Oklahoma, and in other small cities. In the Tulsa riot which occurred in May, 1935, a virtual war was conducted. After hearing an unfounded rumor of an attack on a White woman by a Negro, mobs declared "open season" on Negroes. Homes were looted and burned. Airplanes were used to spy and bomb. When the melee was over, more than fifty Whites and a hundred Negroes had been killed.

Harlem, too, erupted in 1935, with the first of two major riots which were to occur in that section of New York within a decade. Unlike other forms of violence we have discussed, the Harlem Riots of 1935 and 1943 were not battles between races. They were spontaneous outbursts of frustration on the part of Negroes—early examples of the type of riot which developed in the 1960's. These two Harlem riots are treated in the following chapter.

Race riots continued to be a major expression of race hostilities in the next large wave of riots which occurred in 1943 in Detroit, Los Angeles, and Beaumont, Texas. In general these riots were caused by the heightened expectations of the Negro for first-class citizenship; the continuing migrations into the cities with the ensuing problems of lack of housing and increased proximity of the races; the frustration of the Negro over segregation in the armed forces; the recognition in the Negro's mind of the contradiction between the objective of fighting against the Nazis' conceptions of race superiority and his own inferior position in American society; and the White fear of the Negro's supposed super-sexuality.

Nonetheless, each of these riots had notably different characteristics. The riots in Los Angeles, for example, highlighted the racial prejudices of the Caucasian. Called the "Zoot-Suit Riots" because of the type of dress being worn by male Mexican-Americans (and by young males throughout the nation at that time)* they took place in the Mexican-American area of Los Angeles and were racially-oriented clashes.

Most destructive of the Second World War racial confrontations, however, was the Detroit riot which stemmed from discrimination in a housing project and White attitudes toward equal employment rulings. The Negro ghetto of "Paradise Valley" was dilapidated and overcrowded. A new housing development, named after the famous Negro female abolitionist Sojourner Truth, was constructed and designed for war workers. Negroes, however, were essentially excluded from the project. But housing was not the only source of friction between the races in Detroit. The administration of federal regulations requiring equal employment standards in defense and war industries, a regulation stemming from President Franklin D. Roosevelt's significant Executive Order 8802 in which discrimination was prohibited, had angered Whites. In the months prior to the riot, several unauthorized walkouts had occurred in automobile plants, one of them numbering almost 20,000 workers. Several of these "walks" had been prompted by the upgrading of Negro workers. White-supremacist advocates, such as Gerald L. K. Smith, Father Charles Coughlin, and others further stirred prejudicial feeling among White southerners who had also migrated to Detroit since the beginning of the war. A fight began at an amusement park one hot, muggy Sunday evening—and a full-scale riot occurred.

In both the 1935 Harlem and the 1943 Detroit riots, Negroes were aggressive in their retaliatory actions. Having improved their status, growing angry over the contradiction between the objectives of the war as a fight against racism yet discriminated against and segregated in the armed forces, feeling aggrieved over poor housing conditions, Negroes asserted themselves against prejudicial attacks. In Harlem in 1943, the Black people did much more: they rioted against infringements of their rights within their own area.

---

* The zoot-suit outfit featured a jacket approximately thirty-seven inches in length with wide and padded shoulders, trousers full at the knee and narrowly pegged at the cuffs, a long key chain, and sometimes a pancake hat with a small feather in it.

# The Gestapo in Detroit (1943)*

*Thurgood Marshall*

Riots are usually the result of many underlying causes, yet no single factor is more important than the attitude and efficiency of the police. When disorder starts, it is either stopped quickly or permitted to spread into serious proportions, depending upon the actions of the local police.

Much of the blood spilled in the Detroit riot is on the hands of the Detroit police department. In the past the Detroit police have been guilty of both inefficiency and an attitude of prejudice against Negroes. Of course, there are several individual exceptions.

The citizens of Detroit, White and Negro, are familiar with the attitude of the police as demonstrated during the trouble in 1942 surrounding the Sojourner Truth housing project. At that time a mob of White persons armed with rocks, sticks and other weapons attacked Negro tenants who were attempting to move into the project. Police were called to the scene. Instead of dispersing the mob which was unlawfully on property belonging to the federal government and leased to Negroes, they directed their efforts toward dispersing the Negroes who were attempting to get into their own homes. All Negroes approaching the project were searched and their automobiles likewise searched. White people were neither searched nor disarmed by the police. This incident is typical of the one-sided law enforcement practiced by Detroit police. White hoodlums were justified in their belief that the police would act the same way in any further disturbances.

In the June riot of this year, the police ran true to form. The trouble reached riot proportions because the police once again enforced the law with an unequal hand. They used "persuasion" rather than firm action with White rioters, while against Negroes they used the ultimate in force: night sticks, revolvers, riot guns, submachine guns, and deer guns. As a result, twenty-five of the thirty-four persons killed were Negroes. Of the latter, seventeen were killed by police.

The excuse of the police department for the disproportionate number of Negroes killed is that the majority of them were shot while committing felonies; namely, the looting of stores on Hasting Street.

---

* From *The Crisis* (August, 1943), 232–233, 246.

On the other hand, the crimes of arson and felonious assaults are also felonies. It is true that some Negroes were looting stores and were shot while committing these crimes. It is equally true that White persons were turning over and burning automobiles on Woodward Avenue. This is arson. Others were beating Negroes with iron pipes, clubs, and rocks. This is felonious assault. Several Negroes were stabbed. This is assault with intent to murder.

All these crimes are matters of record; many were committed in the presence of police officers, several on the pavement around the City Hall. Yet the record remains: Negroes killed by police—seventeen; White persons killed by police—none. The entire record, both of the riot killings and of previous disturbances, reads like the story of the Nazi Gestapo.

Evidence of tension in Detroit has been apparent for months. The *Detroit Free Press* sent a reporter to the police department. When Commissioner Witherspoon was asked how he was handling the situation he told the reporter: "We have given orders to handle it with kid gloves. The policemen have taken insults to keep trouble from breaking out. I doubt if you or I could have put up with it." This weak-kneed policy of the police commissioner coupled with the anti-Negro attitude of many members of the force helped to make a riot inevitable.

## Sunday Night on Belle Isle

Belle Isle is a municipal recreation park where thousands of White and Negro war workers and their families go on Sundays for their outings. There had been isolated instances of racial friction in the past. On Sunday night, June 20, there was trouble between a group of White and Negro people. The disturbance was under control by midnight. During the time of the disturbance and after it was under control, the police searched the automobiles of all Negroes and searched the Negroes as well. They did not search the white people. One Negro who was to be inducted into the army the following week was arrested because another person in the car had a small penknife. This youth was later sentenced to ninety days in jail before his family could locate him. Many Negroes were arrested during this period and rushed to local police stations. At the very beginning the police demonstrated that they would continue to handle racial disorders by searching, beating and arresting Negroes while using mere persuasion on White people.

## The Riot Spreads

A short time after midnight, disorder broke out in a White neighborhood near the Roxy theatre on Woodward Avenue. The Roxy is an all-night theatre attended by white and Negro patrons. Several Negroes were beaten and others were forced to remain in the theatre for lack of police protection. The rumor spread among the White people that a Negro had raped a White woman on Belle Island and that the Negroes were rioting.

At about the same time a rumor spread around Hastings and Adams Streets in the Negro area that White sailors had thrown a Negro woman and her baby into the lake at Belle Isle and that the police were beating Negroes. This rumor was also repeated by an unidentified Negro at one of the night spots. Some Negroes began to attack White persons in the area. The police immediately began to use their sticks and revolvers against them. The Negroes began to break out the windows of stores of White merchants on Hastings Street.

The interesting thing is that when the windows in the stores on Hastings Street were first broken, there was no looting. An officer of the Merchants' Association walked the length of Hastings Street, starting at seven o'clock Monday morning and noticed that none of the stores with broken windows had been looted. It is thus clear that the original breaking of windows was not for the purpose of looting.

Throughout Monday the police, instead of placing men in front of the stores to protect them from looting, contented themselves with driving up and down Hastings Street from time to time, stopping in front of the stores. The usual procedure was to jump out of the squad cars with drawn revolvers and riot guns to shoot whoever might be in the store. The policemen would then tell the Negro bystanders to "run and not look back." On several occasions, persons running were shot in the back. In other instances, bystanders were clubbed by police. To the police, all Negroes on Hastings Street were "looters." This included war workers returning from work. There is no question that many Negroes were guilty of looting, just as there is always looting during earthquakes or as there was when English towns were bombed by the Germans.

## Cars Detoured into Mobs

Woodward Avenue is one of the main thoroughfares of the city of Detroit. Small groups of White people began to rove up and down Woodward beating Negroes, stoning cars containing Negroes, stopping streetcars and yanking Negroes from them, and stabbing and shooting Negroes. In no case did the police do more than try to "reason" with these mobs, many of which were, at this stage, quite small. The police did not draw their revolvers or riot guns, and never used any force to disperse these mobs. As a result of this, the mobs got larger and bolder and even attacked Negroes on the pavement of the City Hall in demonstration not only of their contempt for Negroes, but of their contempt for law and order as represented by the municipal government.

During this time, Mayor Jeffries was in his office in the City Hall with the door locked and the window shade drawn. The use of night sticks or the drawing of revolvers would have dispersed these White groups and saved the lives of many Negroes. It would not have been necessary to shoot, [as] it would have been sufficient to threaten to shoot into the White mobs. The use of a fire hose would have dispersed many of the groups. None of these things was done and the disorder took on the proportions of a major riot. The responsibility rests with the Detroit police.

At the height of the disorder on Woodward Avenue, Negroes driving north on Brush Street (a Negro street) were stopped at Vernor Highway by a policeman who forced them to detour to Woodward Avenue. Many of these cars are automobiles which appeared in the pictures released by several newspapers showing them overturned and burned on Woodward Avenue.

While investigating the riot, we obtained many affidavits from Negroes concerning police brutality during the riot. It is impossible to include the facts of all of these affidavits. However, typical instances may be cited. A Negro soldier in uniform who had recently been released from the army with a medical discharge, was on his way down Brush Street Monday morning, toward a theatre on Woodward Avenue. This soldier was not aware of the fact that the riot was still going on. While in the Negro neighborhood on Brush Street, he reached a corner where a squad car drove up and discharged several policemen with drawn revolvers who announced to a small group on the corner to run and not look back. Several of the Negroes who did not move quite fast enough for the police were struck with night sticks and revolvers. The soldier was yanked from behind by one policeman and struck in the head with a blunt instrument and knocked to the ground, where he remained in a stupor. The police then returned to their squad car and drove off. A Negro woman in the block noticed the entire incident from her window, and she rushed out with a cold, damp towel to bind the soldier's head. She then hailed two Negro postal employees who carried the soldier to a hospital where his life was saved.

There are many additional affidavits of similar occurrences involving obviously innocent civilians throughout many Negro sections in Detroit where there had been no rioting at all. It was characteristic of these cases that the policemen would drive up to a corner, jump out with drawn revolvers, striking at Negroes indiscriminately, ofttimes shooting at them, and in all cases forcing them to run. At the same time on Woodward Avenue, White civilians were seizing Negroes and telling them to "run, nigger, run." At least two Negroes, "shot while looting," were innocent persons who happened to be in the area at that time.

One Negro who had been an employee of a bank in Detroit for the past eighteen years was on his way to work on a Woodward Avenue streetcar when he was seized by one of the White mobs. In the presence of at least four policemen, he was beaten and stabbed in the side. He also heard several shots fired from the back of the mob. He managed to run to two of the policemen who proceeded to "protect" him from the mob. The two policemen, followed by two mounted policemen, proceeded down Woodward Avenue. While he was being escorted by these policemen, the man was struck in the face by at least eight of the mob, and at no time was any effort made to prevent him from being struck. After a short distance this man noticed a squad car parked on the other side of the street. In sheer desperation, he broke away from the two policemen who claimed to be protecting him and ran to the squad car, begging for protection. The officer in the squad car put him in the back seat and drove off, thereby saving his life.

During all this time, the fact that the man was either shot or stabbed was evident because of the fact that blood was spurting from his side. Despite this obvious felony, committed in the presence of at least four policemen, no effort was made at that time either to protect the victim or to arrest the persons guilty of the felony.

# The Zoot-Suit Riots (1943)*

*Carey McWilliams*

On the evening of Thursday, June 3, the Alpine Club—a group made up of youngsters of Mexican descent—held a meeting in a police sub-station in Los Angeles. They met in the police station, at the invitation of an officer, because of the circumstance that the nearby public school happened to be closed. With a police officer present, they met to discuss their problems, foremost of which, at this meeting, was the urgent question of how best to preserve the peace in their locality. At the conclusion of the meeting, they were taken in squad cars to the street corner nearest the neighborhood in which most of them lived. The squad cars were scarcely out of sight, when the boys were assualted. Thus began the recent week-end race riots in Los Angeles.

On the following nights of June 4, 5 and 6, various attacks were made upon so-called zoot-suiters in Los Angeles. These attacks reached a fine frenzy on Monday evening, June 7, when a mob of a thousand or more soldiers and sailors, with some civilians, set out to round up all zoot-suiters within reach. The mob pushed its way into every important downtown motion-picture theatre, ranged up and down the aisles, and grabbed Mexicans out of their seats. Mexicans and a few Negroes were taken into the streets, beaten, kicked around, their clothing torn. Mobs ranged the length of Main Street in downtown Los Angeles (a distance of some ten or twelve blocks), got as far into the Negro section as Twelfth and Central (just on the edge of the district), and then turned back through the Mexican sections on the east side. Zoot-suiters, so-called, were attacked in the streets, in the theaters, in the bars; street cars were stopped and searched for Mexicans; and boys as young as twelve and thirteen years of age were beaten. Perhaps not more than half the victims were actually wearing zoot-suits. In several cases on Main Street, in downtown Los Angeles, Mexicans were stripped of their clothes and left lying naked on the pavements (front-page pictures of these victims were gleefully displayed in such sedate sheets as the *Los Angeles Times*). During all of this uproar, both regular and special

---

* *The New Republic* (June 21, 1943), 818–820. Reprinted by permission of *The New Republic* (© 1943), Harrison-Blaine of New Jersey, Inc.

police were observed in the streets, outside the theatres, and, in some cases, they were even noted going ahead of the mob. That there was going to be trouble on Main Street on Monday night was known throughout the community for at least twenty-four hours in advance. Crowds collected there, in fact, in anticipation of the fracas. On the following nights the same type of rioting occurred on a smaller scale in Los Angeles, with similar disturbances in Pasadena, Long Beach and San Diego.

Immediate responsibility for the outbreak of the riots must be placed upon the Los Angeles press and the Los Angeles police. For more than a year now the press (and particularly the Hearst press) has been building up anti-Mexican sentiment in Los Angeles. Using the familiar Harlem "crime-wave" technique, the press has headlined every case in which a Mexican has been arrested, featured photographs of Mexicans dressed in "zoot-suits," checked back over the criminal records to "prove" that there has been an increase in Mexican "crime" and constantly needled the police to make more arrests. This campaign reached such a pitch, during the Sleepy Lagoon case in August, 1942, that the Office of War Information sent a representative to Los Angeles to reason with the publishers. The press was most obliging: it dropped the word "Mexican" and began to feature "zoot-suit." The constant repetition of the phrase "zoot-suit," coupled with Mexican names and pictures of Mexicans, had the effect of convincing the public that all Mexicans were zoot-suiters and all zoot-suiters were criminals; ergo, all Mexicans were criminals. On Sunday night and Monday morning (June 6 and 7) stories appeared in the press warning that an armed mob of 500 zoot-suiters was going to engage in acts of retaliation Monday night (thus ensuring a good turnourt for the show that evening).

At the time of the Sleepy Lagoon case last year, the police launched a campaign, which coincided perfectly with the newspaper campaign, against "Mexican crime." Almost on the eve of a speech by Vice-President Wallace in Los Angeles on the good-neighbor policy, police arrested more than 300 Mexican youngsters in what the *Los Angeles Times* referred to as "the biggest roundup since Prohibition days." At about this time, Captain Ayres of the Sheriff's office submitted a report to the Grand Jury in which he characterized the Mexican as being "biologically" predisposed toward criminal behavior. For more than a year this campaign of police terrorization has continued. Prowl cars have been cruising through the Mexican section constantly; youngsters have been ordered off the streets and "frisked' whenever two or more have been found together; and persistent complaints of police brutality have issued from both the Mexican and Negro communities. There are, of course, some fine officers on the force—men who know and understand the problem. To some extent, also, the police have been goaded into the use of repressive measures by the press and by the race-baiting of some local officials. The manner in which the problem of the Japanese evacuees has been kept before the public, for example, has had a tendency to make people race-conscious. Nor have some local officials yet changed their attitudes. "Mayor Pledges Two-Fisted Action, No Wrist Slap," reads a headline in the *Los Angeles Examiner* (June 10). At the same time, the attitude of certain military officials has, also, been rather shocking.

The "official" version of the riots, adopted by all the major newspapers, is now as follows: the soldiers and sailors acted in self-defense and, most emphatically, there was no element of race prejudice involved ("ZOOT-SUIT GANGSTERS PLAN WAR ON NAVY"—headline, *Los Angeles Daily News*, June 8, 1943). This theory is desperately repeated, despite the fact that *only Mexicans and Negroes* were singled out for attack. As for prejudice against *Mexicans*—from whom we acquired so many elements of our "culture"—why, the very suggestion of such a thought would seem to be abhorrent to the postriot conscience of every publisher in Los Angeles. In fact, the fanciest journalistic double-talk that I have seen in the Los Angeles press during a residence of twenty-one years, appeared in the editorials of June 11.

Several facts need to be rather dogmatically asserted:

1) There are no "zoot-suit" gangs in Los Angeles in the criminal sense of the word "gang." The *pachuco* "gangs" are loosely organized neighborhood or geographical groups; they are not tied together into an "organization." Many of them are, in effect, nothing more than boys' clubs without a clubhouse.

2) Juvenile delinquency has increased in Los Angeles since the war, but while delinquency among Mexican youth has risen as part of this general situation, it has actually increased less than that of other ethnic groups and less than the citywide average for all groups.

3) Much of the miscellaneous crime that the newspapers have been shouting about has been committed, not by youngsters, but by men.

4) While individual Mexicans may, in a few cases, have at-tacked soldiers and sailors (and, incidentally, the reverse of this proposition is true), it is merely the craziest nonsense to suggest that the soldiers and sailors were driven to mob violence in self-defense.

5) It should be kept in mind that about 98 per cent of Mexi-can youth in Los Angeles is American-born, American-raised, American-educated. Like most second-generation immigrant groups, they have their special problems. But their actual record for law observance is, all things considered, exceptionally good.

While the riots have now subsided (business has been complaining about the cancellation of military leaves), the situation itself has not been corrected. In the absence of a full and open investigation, the public has been left with the general impression (1) that the soldiers and sailors acted in self-defense; and (2) that, all things considered, the riots were "wholesome" and had a "good effect." Resentment of the riots in the Mexican and Negro communities has reached an intensity and bitterness that could not be exaggerated.

Chapter Four

# The Harlem Riots: Violence of the Future

The two Harlem riots which occurred within a seven-year period in the decades of the 1930's and 1940's represent a different type of group violence, a type which presaged the riots of the 1960's. In both of the riots, the participants were primarily Black and the action was contained within the Harlem ghetto. Both riots involved only Whites who were seen as symbols of repression, such as the police, or those who were unfortunate enough to be in the area when the riot began. Both upheavals commenced with an episode which was expanded by rumors, the rumors in content and effect again reflecting a prejudiced society. Both incidents flared in troubled times; the first occurred during the Great Depression which adversely affected millions of Negroes living in heavily concentrated large metropolitan areas of the North and Midwest, the next one ensuing during the Second World War.

There were differences between the two Harlem riots. The violence of 1935 occurred at a time when hundreds of thousands of Negroes were out of work and unable to find employment, often due to discrimination. A saying in the Negro community gave pointed evidence to their intense pique: "The Negro is the last to be hired, and the first to be fired." Housing was wretched; hunger affected many children and the elderly; rents were too high; and conditions were deplorable. In the 1940's, the war brought many more Negroes and Caucasians into closer and more intensified contact. The 1943 riot grew out of innumerable instances of personal insult paid the Negroes in the wartime society. Thousands of Black soldiers were forced to suffer indignities through-out the country. It is significant that it was the shooting of a Negro soldier by a White policeman in the lobby of a Harlem hotel that incited the violence.

In both of these riots in Harlem, the aggression of the Blacks was directed towards the destruction of property and the looting of stores. Several percep-tive observers anticipated that this type of riot would later predominate. Wit-ness this statement in Myrdal's *An American Dilemma:* "If these [outbreaks] occur, they will be due to continuing discrimination from the Whites and to the growing realization by Negroes that peaceful requests for their rights are not getting them anywhere." ·

In 1964, the third major Harlem riot of the twentieth century repeated the theme of the 1935 and 1943 riots and introduced the style of violence the nation was to experience in the 1960's: the protest riot.

# The Riot of 1935*

*Hamilton Basso*

Lino Rivera is a Puerto Rican Negro who is sixteen years old. He lives in Harlem and has no job. He sometimes runs errands for a Harlem theatre and has done other odd jobs. On the afternoon of March 19, after attending a motion-picture show, he went into a Kress store on West One Hundred and Twenty-fifth Street, one of Harlem's principal thoroughfares. He passed a counter displaying hardware and saw a knife he liked. The knife cost ten cents. Rivera decided to lift it and slipped it in his pocket. A clerk saw him and took the knife away. He held the boy by the arm and began to push him out of the store. The boy said:

"I can walk. You don't have to push me."

"Don't talk back," the clerk answered. "You ought to be glad I'm not going to have you arrested."

The clerk continued to push the boy and Rivera protested again. A small crowd gathered around them.

"I told you not to push me," the boy said.

"Don't get fresh," the clerk said. "If you do, I'll call a cop."

---

* *The New Republic* (April 3, 1935), 209–210. Reprinted by permission of *The New Republic* (© 1935), Harrison-Blaine of New Jersey, Inc.

"What's he done?" asked a woman in the crowd.

"I ain't done nothing," the boy said.

"The hell you haven't," said the clerk.

A second clerk came up and now the two of them began to struggle with the boy. He clung to a post and began to kick at the two men who tried to pull him away. The crowd became larger. Voices rose in protest.

"What they fighting with that boy for?"

"What you done, boy?"

"I ain't done nothing," the boy shouted.

"They ain't got no right to treat that boy that way."

The two men pulled the boy from the post and began to drag him away. The boy fought and kicked and bit. He bit one of the men on the thumb and the other on the wrist. The man who was bitten on the thumb began to bleed. He shouted: "I'm going to take you down to the basement and beat hell out of you."

The boy was taken to the basement, still fighting with his captors, but less violently now, and a conference was held with a few policemen who had appeared. It was decided, finally, to let the boy go free. He was taken to the back door and turned loose. He ran straight home.

Meanwhile, in the store, the anger and resentment of the crowd had mounted. A woman screamed that they were beating the boy to death and that rumor, spreading, reached a second crowd that had gathered before the store. Threats of violence began to be heard. A speaker started to address the crowd. Policemen reached the scene and tried to break up the gathering. The people refused to move. The speaker continued his harangue. He urged the people to hold their ground.

In the store, now a scene of considerable confusion, the crowd waited for the boy to reappear. He did not and the notion that he was being beaten in the basement seemed to be confirmed. Men in the crowd suggested that they go and free the boy. Women became hysterical. In the excitement a counter was turned over. Some of the employees, becoming frightened at the temper of the crowd, began to leave.

Then, its siren shrieking through the streets, an ambulance stopped before the store. It had been called for the man whose finger had been bitten, but the crowd, its anger growing every minute, thought that it had come to take the boy to the hospital. It began to surge into the store. Three other speakers had joined the first orator and one of them had mounted a ladder. A policeman started toward the man on the ladder and the first fighting began.

With the appearance of the ambulance, the crowd was convinced that the boy had been brutally beaten. It was now well out of hand and the policemen on duty sent in a call for reinforcements. A brick crashed through a window. The spread of splintering glass was lost in the roar of the crowd. And then, further to substantiate the idea that the boy had been beaten, a hearse appeared. Now it was believed that the boy had been killed. The crowd, yelling with rage, poured into the store.

It was about this time, perhaps an hour and a half after the boy was first caught, that leaflets were circulated through the crowd. These leaflets, mimeographed, were worded as follows:

CHILD BRUTALLY BEATEN
WOMAN ATTACKED BY BOSS AND COPS
CHILD NEAR DEATH

One hour ago a twelve-year-old Negro boy was brutally beaten by the management of Kress's Five and Ten Cent Store.

Boy is near death. He was mercilessly beaten because they thought he had "stolen" a five-cent knife.

A Negro woman who sprang to the defense of the boy has had arms broken by these thugs and was then arrested.

Workers! Negro and White!

Protest against this lynch attack on innocent Negro People!

Demand the release of the boy and the woman!

Demand the immediate arrest of the manager responsible for this lynch attack!

Don't buy at Kress's!

Stop police brutality in Harlem!

ISSUED BY YOUNG LIBERATORS.

How much these leaflets contributed to the trouble cannot be determined. The opinion in Harlem, after the riot, was that they contributed a great deal. Their appearance, regardless of who was responsible for them, was certainly thoughtless and ill advised. With the crowd already in a sullen mood, with the air full of threats and wild rumors, the positive statement that the boy had been brutally beaten, along with a woman who tried to help him, was not likely to restore any calm or reason. It may be said that the flare-up in Harlem would have occurred whether they were distributed or not. It is equally true, however, that the trouble reached the proportions of a riot, and a race riot, only after they were placed in the hands of the crowd.

To believe, however, that the purpose of these leaflets was deliberately to provoke a race riot, that it was carefully calculated and planned by the Communists, is to believe in the stupid Red scare of the Hearst press. That they helped to rouse the crowds to violence is true. That the violence might have been less if they had not appeared is also true. But not they, or any other leaflet, would have precipitated such trouble if Harlem had not already been smoldering with anger and resentment.

To begin with, Harlem is from 55 to 60 per cent unemployed. Many of its inhabitants, before the Depression, were employed as house servants or as attendants in hotels. Others worked in the building trades, as elevator men, as waiters and dishwashers in restaurants. Not all Harlem Negroes, contrary to the impression to be gained from a number of novels, are orchestra leaders and nightclub entertainers. They have been hit perhaps harder than any other group in New York. Many of them have not had work in four years.

Relief has been inadequate. Charges have been made that it is one-third lower in Harlem than elsewhere. Some unemployed Negroes say they have to wait days, and some say weeks, before getting assistance. Relief administration has been entirely in the hands White persons whose knowledge and understanding of the Negro is limited. White investigators have caused much antagonism and bad feeling. There have been quarrels and recriminations and, in some instances, fist-fights and brawls.

As a result of the Depression, Negro families have been forced to combine their resources and live together. Congestion and miserable living conditions have resulted. While there is no legal restriction of Negroes to any one district in New York City they are forced to live in Harlem because landlords in other parts of the city refuse to rent to them. Harlem landlords have taken advantage of this situation to raise rents to exorbitant heights. It is common knowledge that an apartment worth $25 rents for $40 or even $50 in Harlem. Some of these apartments have not been renovated or improved in years. Many of them even lack toilet conveniences.

A certain portion of the Harlem population, during the boom, was relatively prosperous. During 1919 and 1920, Negroes living in Harlem took title to over $5 million worth of real estate. Most of this investment has been lost. One Negro leader in Harlem states that there is hardly a bank in New York that will renew mortgages on property owned or occupied by Negroes; and, if they are renewed, the rate of interest charged is higher than that charged to Whites.

The greatest cause of resentment is the discrimination shown in the matter of employment. Many stores in Harlem will not employ Negro help, chief among these being the three large five-and-ten-cent stores on One Hundred and Twenty-fifth Street. As a protest against this, boycotting organizations have been formed, among them the Negro Industrial and Clerical Alliance and the Citizens' Committee for Fair Play. These organizations, by use of the boycott, seek to get jobs for the members of their organizations in those stores discriminating against the Negro.

It was these things that formed the background of the Harlem riot. One Negro, in discussing the affair, said he was surprised that trouble had not broken out before this. It has been brewing for a long time. The chance apprehension of a boy, the spread of a rumor that seemed to have a basis in fact, was only the accident that set off the anger of a section of society that has suffered through five years of depression. If the New York City government wishes to prevent a recurrence of the Harlem riot, it had best go to the root of the trouble and not attempt to place the onus of a tragic incident upon any one radical group.


# Behind the Harlem Riot of 1943*

*Walter White*


A few weeks before Harlem burst into flames on Sunday night, August 1, a young Negro who had just received his gold bars from an Officers' Candidate School in a southern state came to see me. His face beamed with modest pride and love of country as he told of raising his hand to take the oath as an officer of the United States Army to protect his country with his life.

"Ten minutes later I boarded the bus to Washington along with some of my fellow officers—White boys from Georgia, Mississippi and

* *The New Republic* (August 16, 1943), 220–222. Reprinted by permission of *The New Republic* (© 1945), Harrison-Blaine of New Jersey, Inc.

Arkansas. We were all so excited and happy over winning our commissions that I forgot we were still in the South," he said. His trim, immaculately clad body sagged and a cloud came over his face as he told me of what happened then.

"Hey, all nigras sit in the back of the bus!" the bus driver yelled at him.

"I made up my mind right then that I had taken the last insult from crackers I was going to take," the Negro officer told me grimly.

"If I had to die for democracy, I decided that there was no better time or place than right then. I told the driver I was not going to sit in any Jim Crow section and that if he was man enough to make me do so, he would have to do it. I sat down in the 'White' section and rode into Washington."

No clash or tragedy occurred in this instance, possibly because the White southern campanions of the Negro officer came to his defense. But multiply this episode by many thousands. Include in it the story of New York's famed 369th Regiment which has done an excellent job as an anti-aircraft unit "somewhere in the Pacific." Two hundred and twelve picked officers and men were returned to the United States to act as cadres in the training of new units. They were sent to Camp Stewart, Georgia, where, in the camp as well as on buses going into Savannah and in Savannah itself, a long succession of indignities were heaped upon these men to "teach these northern Negroes their place."

Naturally these soldiers wrote to their relatives and friends in New York. Harlem newspapers published the stories. They became another segment of many other tales from southern camps such as the killing by a Louisiana state policeman of Raymond Carr, a Negro MP, when Carr refused to leave his post of duty at the order of a White civil policeman. Only after enormous pressure was the policeman punished. His punishment consisted of a one-day suspension.

Last May 29 Judge William H. Hastie and Thurgood Marshall submitted a report on civilian violence against Negro soldiers to the National Lawyers' Guild, which in turn formally placed it before the War and Justice Departments. It was pointed out that recurrent violence in the civilian community directed against Negro members of the armed forces had increased in seriousness, in frequency and in the lack of any effective methods of control since a similar study had been made in November, 1942. The report grimly stated:

Civilian violence against the Negro in uniform is a recurrent phenomenon. It continues unabated. It may well be the greatest factor now operating to make 13 million Negroes bitter and resentful and to undermine the fighting spirit of three-quarters of a million Negroes in arms. Yet, no effective steps are being taken and no vigorous, continuing and comprehensive program of action has been inaugurated by state or federal authorities to stamp out this evil. . . . To address a Negro soldier as "nigger" is such a commonplace in the average southern community that little is said about it. But the mounting rage of the soldier himself is far from commonplace. He may not express his feelings when he must wait until all the white passengers are accommodated before he can get transportation. He may even hold his tongue when he is forced to get out of the bus in which he is seated in order to make room for white passengers. But it is of such stuff that bitterness and hatred are made. In such a climate resentments grow until they burst forth in violent and unreasoning reprisal.

This prophetic statement is carefully documented with specific instances similar to the Raymond Carr case. Among them was recited the killing of Sergeant Thomas Foster, a Negro soldier, in March, 1943, by a city policeman in the streets of Little Rock, Arkansas. Foster was shot and killed while lying dazed on the ground. After killing Foster, the policeman calmly returned his revolver to its holster, took out his pipe and lit it. In July, 1942, city police officers of Beaumont, Texas, fired several shots into the body of a Negro soldier, Private Charles Reco, who had been arrested on complaint of a bus driver because Reco sat under a sign dividing the seating between Whites and Negroes. His body was behind the sign in the Jim Crow section; his knees in front of it. To avoid trouble, Reco left the bus and was overtaken by the policeman, who hit him with a blackjack from behind and then fired into his prostrate body. Attorney-General Francis Biddle issued a strong statement and promised vigorous federal action. But later the Department of Justice abandoned prosecution because there was "no prospect of conviction." The Guild Report adds wryly: "This is not the first time that the Department of Justice has lost its ardor for action in Texas. In the circumstances, we can only hope that the extraordinary power of the Texas delegate to Congress has no relationship to the mental vagaries of the Department of Justice."

Other killings of Negro soldiers were cited in El Paso, Texas; Mobile, Alabama; Columbia, South Carolina; and other places.

It is out of this sad record that the shooting, not without justification, of Robert J. Brandy, a Negro MP, in a Harlem hotel by a White policeman on Sunday night, August 1, provided the spark which set off the explosion created by bitter, smoldering resentment against the mistreatment of Negro soldiers which was all the more dangerous because it had been pent up and frustrated. A five-minute shift in Private Bandy's movements that sultry Sunday might have averted one of the most destructive riots in American history, which took a toll of five lives, injured 307 and caused damage estimated to be in excess of $5 million. Bandy came to New York from a New Jersey camp to meet his mother, who had come down from Middletown, Connecticut, to spend Sunday with him and his fiancee. Bandy's mother checked out of the hotel around four o'clock in the afternoon and then set out with her son and his friend for dinner and a moving-picture show. It was an unfortunate, gratuitous circumstance that they returned to the hotel to pick up the mother's luggage just as an altercation developed when a policeman sought to eject an obstreperous Negro woman.

Bandy intervened, so the story goes, in an attempt to defend the woman. During the altercation he is alleged to have seized Policeman James Collins' night stick and to have struck the policeman across the cheekbone. He then turned away, refusing to obey the order to halt. The policeman drew his gun and fired, hitting Bandy in the left shoulder. Within a few minutes, the story had spread like wildfire throughout Harlem that a Negro soldier had been shot in the back and killed by a policeman in the presence of his mother. Blind, unreasoning fury swept the community with the speed of lightning. The available symbols of the oppressor, as was the case in Detroit's East Side [1943], were the shining plate-glass windows of stores along One Hundred and Twenty-fifth Street. At the beginning, there was no looting. Nothing but blind fury was expressed. Later, from the more poverty-stricken areas of Harlem, poured those who entered the stores through the broken windows and began looting. Their acts were criminal and unforgivable. But let him who would criticize pause long enough to put himself in the place of the looters. Still barred from many defense industries in the area because of color, with dark memories of the Depression years when 70 per cent of Harlem was on relief because Negroes are hired last and there were not enough jobs for White workers, hemmed in a ghetto where they are forced to pay disproportionately high rents for rat- and vermin-infested apartments, the Bigger Thomases of New York passed like a cloud of locusts over the stores of Harlem.

But the usual pattern of riots did not obtain. I spent the night touring the district with Mayor LaGuardia, Police Commissioner Valentine and residents of the Harlem community. Mayor LaGuardia was on the scene a few minutes after the trouble started and remained there, as did Commissioner Valentine, without sleep or sufficient food until daybreak Tuesday.

The Mayor and the Police Commissioner did not content themselves with bringing in policemen and anti-mob paraphernalia. Even before the policemen poured in, Mayor LaGuardia called all the leaders of public opinion in Harlem who could be reached. A small board of strategy was set up. One of the first steps taken was to request the army to send Negro as well as White MP's into the area, and to have them perform their duties of rounding up military personnel in the riot area, in mixed units instead of separate ones. This had a calming effect on the community.

All during the night Negroes known to the people of Harlem broadcast from sound trucks exploding the false rumor that Bandy had been killed and urging the people to return to their homes and to stop vandalism and other violent acts. Coupled with this was the magnificent restraint and efficiency of the police. Daylight saw the diminution of violence. An exhausted community, its fury spent, was shocked at the damage done. Decent members of the community, most of whom had slept through the night unaware of what had taken place, were appalled. Condemnation far more severe than any person outside the community could utter was voiced in increasing volume throughout Harlem against the acts of irresponsible, criminal persons.

How different was Detroit! There a weak Mayor hid while Negroes were beaten on the steps of the City Hall itself. New York's Mayor was in the thick of the trouble, often at great personal risk. During the early morning hours, a report came to the Twenty-eighth Precinct in One Hundred and Twenty-third Street that a mob of Whites was forming down near the New York Central's One Hundred and Twenty-fifth Street station. Refusing to wait long enough for Police Commissioner Valentine to supply him with a patrol car of policemen to protect him, the ebullient Mayor bundled me into a one-seater police car in which we were sped to the section. We found the rumor to be utterly false.

Returning, we came through Lenox Avenue, where there was looting. Regardless of personal danger, the Mayor shouted, "Put that stuff down," to a group of youthful vandals. Utterly startled, they dropped what they had in their hands and fled.

New York's Police Commissioner Lewis J. Valentine provided an equally sharp contrast to Detroit's Commissioner Witherspoon. Even more remarkable was the attitude of the police themselves. All during Sunday night and early Monday morning, thousands of police poured into the Twenty-eighth Precinct straight from eight hours of duty. Prior to being sent out on the streets they were herded into an insufferably hot squad room where a single drinking fountain served us all. During all those troubled hours, I heard not one word about "niggers," as I had heard so frequently in Detroit, nor was there any other manifestation of racial animosity. They were out to do a job of restoring order, and it was all in the day's work.

But though New York City acquitted itself nobly and established a pattern of procedure which should guide both it and other cities in future outbreaks, stopping a riot quickly and efficiently is only a small part of the problem involved. The weight of sustained and unceasing public opinion must activate the federal government, and particularly the Army, the Navy and the Department of Justice, to stop, at whatever cost, the unchecked brutality against Negro servicemen which has cursed the country. Within the various cities themselves, ghettos must be abolished, along with the evils attendant upon segregation and proscription.

New York had another riot in 1935. Mayor LaGuardia appointed a biracial commission which held hearings and submitted a report which included recommendations that might have prevented, or at least made less likely and less destructive, the riot of August, 1943. But unfortunately, the report was never made public and most of its recommendations were unheeded. It is to be hoped that this mistake will not be made again.

# PART TWO

# PROTEST RIOTS

From the end of World War II until 1964, there were several large-scale urban disturbances which reflected the underlying potential of social violence. None of these conflicts expanded into major urban conflagrations. Rather, most of the clashes were manifestations of Negro challenges to the socio-economic structure of a community. The most intense violence occurred when minority groups attempted to change the residential patterns or when a number of Caucasians defined the situation as one in which such an attempt was being made.

Several urban racial clashes were instigated by Caucasians who resented attempts by Negroes to move into all-White neighborhoods. The Airport Homes violence in Chicago in November, 1946; the Fernwood Project violence in Chicago in August, 1947; the Georgia house-bombings in May, 1947; the publicized Cicero, Illinois violence of 1951; and others, were all Caucasian-initiated hostile responses. Between 1945 and 1948 there were more than a hundred attacks on the persons and property of Negroes who moved, or who attempted to move, out of the Black ghettos into other areas.

Racial violence likewise occurred when Negroes attempted to use public recreational facilities reserved for Caucasians in southern cities like St. Louis, Baltimore, and Washington, D.C., in 1949. Two years later, in Philadelphia, Negroes launched an attack upon discrimination in city construction projects by picketing public buildings, the Mayor's office and home, staging an all-night sit-in in the Mayor's reception room, and battling with police sent to open their picket lines. Many persons were injured and a White minister who participated in the protest was killed. At that time, George Schermer, executive director of Philadelphia's Commission on Human Relations, commented on the lack of communication between city officials and Negroes: "What the Mayor doesn't realize is that when you talk [only] to the thirty or forty most secure and politically sophisticated Negroes in town, you haven't really talked to Negroes at all."

A decade later, the northern, midwestern and western urban areas which contained millions of non-Whites were in flames. In 1964, the northern ghettos spontaneously exploded, bringing scenes of looting, burning, bloodshed, chaos, and bewilderment to an essentially White, affluent society. The rioting began in Harlem when a seasoned police lieutenant shot and killed a Negro youth as the later allegedly lunged at him with a knife. It quickly spread to the Bedford-Stuyvesant section of Brooklyn, an area which houses more Negroes than Harlem, and Negroes in other cities followed suit. In that year the Black masses rioted in Rochester, Trenton, Jersey City, Elizabeth, Patterson, Chicago and Philadelphia. A year later, the forty-square-mile area which surrounded the Black ghetto called Watts in Los Angeles was cordoned off by thousands of police and troops. The Puerto Ricans living in East Harlem and the Negroes again in many cities across the country revolted in 1966. Then in 1967, two of the largest riots in the nation's history occurred in Newark and Detroit; and there was rioting in many other cities as well. In all, there were at least thirty-one riots in the incredibly short space of three years. The week after the assassination of the Reverend Martin Luther King in April, 1968, more rioting took place as Blacks across the country protested individually and collectively.

What produced these riots? What factors coalesced in the 1960's to bring about one of the most serious domestic social crises in American history? The series of articles in the first part of this section focuses on the central factors which brought on the violence. The last part of the section describes the four major riots of the sixties: Harlem, Watts, Newark and Detroit, and discusses the consensus of non-White attitudes born from feelings of alienation and powerlessness.

The protest riots were the actions of a people, poor and crushed together in large slum ghettos, who rose up in wrath against an affluent, indifferent society. Though their outbursts strongly suggest class antagonism, the lower classes protested because of a betrayal: the betrayal of expectations. Enticed by advertising, the mass media, pronouncements by political officials about the "War on Poverty," the poor, non-Whites anticipated imminent improvement in their socioeconomic position. The failure of American society to raise the status of those trapped in the inner areas of the cities resulted in the spontaneous, violent demonstrations against the majority.

# Chapter Five

# The Causes of the
# Protest Riots of the 1960's

The central factors which brought on the violence were the failure of the city as a "Promised Land"; racism in American society; the existence of separate racial worlds; the behavior of the police; the feelings of frustration and the inability of minority groups to bring about political and economic change; and the developing sense of minority identity.

Other legacies of the past contributed to the explosion. Clearly, a high percentage of unemployment, poor housing, crowded living conditions and economic exploitation, as well as hopelessness made the ghetto residents angry and bitter. What made their plight the more visible was the fact that non-Whites, mainly Caucasians, enjoyed an affluence beyond the reach of the minority groups. Moreover, the techniques of the powerful Civil Rights Movement which had brought about several significant changes in the South could not be used to bear upon the complex problems of the northern and western cities. A sense of "invisibility," to use the word in Ralph Ellison's novel *Invisible Man** pervaded the ghetto people.

Each of the riots which took place in the 1960's was characterized by a

---

* Ralph Ellison, *Invisible Man* (New York: Random House, 1952).

widespread desperation. In every aspect of his life, the non-White felt that the power structure mitigated against him. The channels for social redress were largely closed. The riots of the sixties, then, would appear to be the result of release and rebellion against the past—a protest against centuries of being the outsider in America.

# The Civil Rights Commission Report (1959): "An Ancient Warning"*

Soon after his election to the presidency in 1948, Harry S. Truman created a Commission on Civil Rights. The purpose of the body was to examine problems attending race relations. The Commission explored many areas including employment, housing, education, voting, social relations and issued many superb reports. The reports generally concluded that race discrimination was seriously undermining the social fabric of the nation. In fact, in its 1959 report —six years before the explosion in the ghetto areas—the Commission specifically warned "against the division of society into Two Cities." Nearly a decade later, President Lyndon B. Johnson's National Advisory Commission on Civil Disorders wrote and warned of the same division: "This is our basic conclusion: Our nation is moving toward two societies, one Black, one White— separate and unequal."

Few persons paid attention to the fears of the Commission on Civil Rights in 1959—as evidenced by subsequent urban violence on a massive scale.

Through its studies of three particular aspects of civil rights— voting, education, and housing—the Commission has come to see the organic nature of the problem as a whole. The problem is one of securing the full rights of citizenship to those Americans who are being denied in any degree that vital recognition of human dignity, the equal protection of the laws.

To a large extent this is now a racial problem. In the past there was widespread denial of equal opportunity and equal justice by reason of religion or national origin. Some discrimination against Jews remains, particularly in housing, and some recent immigrants undoubtedly still have to overcome prejudice. But with a single exception the only denials of the right to vote that have come to the attention of the Commission are by reason of race or color. This is also

* From the Report of the Civil Rights Commission (1959), pp. 545-547.

clearly the issue in public education. In housing, too, it is primarily non-Whites who lack equal opportunity. Therefore, the Commission has concentrated its studies on the status of the 18 million Negro American citizens, who constitute this country's largest racial minority.[1] If a way can be found to secure and protect the civil rights of this minority group, if a way can be opened for them to finish moving up from slavery to the full human dignity of first-class citizenship, then America will be well on its way toward fulfilling the great promises of the Constitution.

In part this is the old problem of the vicious circle. Slavery, discrimination, and second-class citizenship have demoralized a considerable portion of those suffering these injustices, and the consequent demoralization is then seen by others as a reason for continuing the very conditions that caused the demoralization.

The fundamental interrelationships among the subjects of voting, education, and housing make it impossible for the problem to be solved by the improvement of any one factor alone. If the right to vote is secured, but there is not equal opportunity in education and housing, the value of that right will be discounted by apathy and ignorance. If compulsory discrimination is ended in public education but children continue to be brought up in slums and restricted areas of racial concentration, the conditions for good education and good citizenship will still not obtain.

If decent housing is made available to non-Whites on equal terms but their education and habits of citizenship are not raised, new neighborhoods will degenerate into slums.

.        .        .        .        .        .        .        .        .        .

At its worst, the problem involves a massive demoralization of a considerable part of the non-White population. This is the legacy of generations of slavery, discrimination, and second-class citizenship. Through the vote, education, better housing, and other improving

---

[1] The Commission has not been unmindful of somewhat similar problems faced by the 797,000 Puerto Ricans in the continental U.S. (*Facts and Figures*, April 1958 edition, Migration Division, Department of Labor, Commonwealth of Puerto Rico); the 259,397 Oriental Americans (1950 Census Report P-B 1, Bureau of Census); the 2,281,710 Spanish and Mexican Americans in Arizona, California, Colorado, New Mexico and Texas (1950 Census, Report P-E, No. 3C, Bureau of the Census); and the 469,900 American Indians (1957 estimate of U.S. Public Health Service, Indian Health Branch). Some State Advisory Committees were able to give considerable attention to these problems. A more comprehensive study of them is indicated.

standards of living, American Negroes have made massive strides up from slavery. But many of them, along with many Puerto Rican, Mexican, and Oriental Americans, are still being denied equal opportunity to develop their full potential as human beings.

The pace of progress during the ninety-six years since emancipation has been remarkable. But this is an age of revolutionary change. The Colored peoples of Asia and Africa, constituting a majority of the human race, are swiftly coming into their own. The non-Colored peoples of the world are now on test. The future peace of the world is at stake.

Moreover, science and technology have opened new realms of freedom. In the present competition with the Soviet Union and world communism the United States cannot afford to lose the potential intelligence and skill of any section of its population.

Equal opportunity and equal justice under law must be achieved in all sections of American public life with all deliberate speed. It is not a court of law alone that tells us this, but also the needs of the nation in the light of the clear and present dangers and opportunities facing us, and in the light of our restive national conscience. Time is essential in resolving any great and difficult problem, and more time will be required to solve this one. However, it is not time alone that helps, but the constructive use of time.

The whole problem will not be solved without high vision, serious purpose, and imaginative leadership. Prohibiting discrimination in voting, education, housing, or other parts of our public life will not suffice. The demoralization of a part of the non-White population resulting from generations of discrimination can ultimately be overcome only by positive measures. The law is not merely a command and government is not just a policeman. Law must be inventive, creative, and educational.

To eliminate discrimination and demoralization, some dramatic and creative intervention by the leaders of our national life is necessary. In the American system much of the action needed should come from private enterprise and voluntary citizens' groups and from local and state governments. If they fail in their responsibilities, the burden falls unduly on the federal government.

This Commission would add only one further suggestion. The fundamental cause of prejudice is hidden in the minds and hearts of men. That prejudice will not be cured by concentrating constantly on the discrimination. It may be cured, or reduced, or at least forgotten, if sights can be raised to new and challenging targets. Thus, a curriculum designed to educate young Americans for this unfolding twentieth-century world, with better teachers and better schools, will go a long way to facilitate the transition in public education. Equal opportunity in housing will come more readily as part of a great program of urban reconstruction and regeneration. The right to vote will more easily be secured throughout the whole South if there are great issues on which people want to vote.

What is involved here is the ancient warning against the division of society into Two Cities. The Constitution of the United States, which was ordained to establish one society with equal justice under law, stands against such a division. America, which already has come closer to equality of opportunity than probably any other country, must succeed where others have failed. It can do this not only by resolving to end discrimination but also by creating through works of faith in freedom a clear and present vision of the City of Man, the one city of free and equal man envisioned by the Constitution.

# Disillusioned Colored Pioneers in the Promised Land (1965)*

*Claude Brown*

Manchild in the Promised Land is the story of Brown's life in Harlem. As a child, Claude Brown attended a school for the emotionally disturbed, and was later sent to a reform school. Changing his style of life, he graduated from Howard University in 1965 and went into politics. At the time, Brown stated that his ambition was to unseat Adam Clayton Powell.

I want to talk about the first northern urban generation of Negroes. I want to talk about the experiences of a misplaced generation, of a misplaced people in an extremely complex, confused society. This is a story of their searching, their dreams, their sorrows, their small and

* Reprinted with permission of The Macmillan Company from *Manchild in the Promised Land* by Claude Brown. Copyright © by Claude Brown, 1965. Distribution rights for the British Commonwealth and Empire granted by Jonathan Cape Ltd.

futile rebellions, and their endless battle to establish their own place in America's greatest metropolis—and in America itself.

The characters are sons and daughters of former southern share-croppers. These were the poorest people of the South who poured into New York City during the decade following the Great Depression. These migrants were told that unlimited opportunities for prosperity existed in New York and that there was no "color problem" there. They were told that Negroes lived in houses with bathrooms, electricity, running water, and indoor toilets. To them, this was the "promised land" that Mammy had been singing about in the cotton fields for many years.

Going back to New York was good-bye to the cotton fields, good-bye to "Massa Charlie," good-bye to the chain gang, and, most of all, good-bye to the sunup-to-sundown working hours. One no longer had to wait to get to heaven to lay his burden down; burdens could be laid down in New York.

So, they came, from all parts of the South, like all the black chillun o' God following the sound of Gabriel's horn on that long-overdue Judgment Day. The Georgians came as soon as they were able to pick train fare off the peach trees. They came from South Carolina where the cotton stalks were bare. The North Carolinians came with tobacco tar beneath their fingernails.

They felt as the Pilgrims must have felt when they were coming to America. But these descendants of Ham must have been twice as happy as the Pilgrims, because they had been catching twice the hell. Even while planning the trip, they sang spirituals as "Jesus Take My Hand" and "I'm On My Way" and chanted, "Hallelujah, I'm on my way to the promised land."

It seems that Cousin Willie, in his lying haste, had neglected to tell the folks down home about one of the most important aspects of the promised land: it was a slum ghetto. There was a tremendous difference in the way that life was lived up north. There were too many people full of hate and bitterness crowded into dirty, stinky, uncared-for closet-size section of a great city.

Before the soreness of the cotton fields had left Mama's back, her knees were getting sore from scrubbing "Goldberg's" floor. Never-theless, she was better off; she had gone from the fire into the frying pan.

The children of these disillusioned Colored pioneers inherited the total lot of their parents—the disappointments, the anger. To add to their misery, they had little hope of deliverance. For where does one run to when he's already in the promised land?

# The Turn to Violence (1968)*

*James E. Alsbrook*

At almost midnight, three Negro boys walked silently through an alley near a furniture store. Bricks in hand, they looked up and down the well-lighted street, threw the bricks through two large plate-glass windows and ran like scared rabbits.

"I feel better now," one said when they slowed to a trot several blocks away. "We got even with that peckerwood," another said.

The place was Kansas City, Kansas. The time was before World War II, and I was one of the boys.

Our neighborhood was not a slum or ghetto. It was quiet, with grassy lawns and single-family homes. Strong father-figures and male breadwinners were in each of our homes. We played with neighborhood White boys nearly every day. Our grandparents had been in the North since the 1880's. My mother was a public schoolteacher and church organist.

Why did we strictly reared boys of the so-called middle class suddenly and deliberately violate firm rules that had been pounded into us at home, at school and at church?

We didn't really know. We told ourselves we were "getting even." That white merchant was advertising mattresses by showing life-size paintings of plantation "niggers" happily picking cotton and eating watermelon. We had asked him to remove them and he laughed, calling us a word we never heard before—"pickaninnies."

We couldn't explain to ourselves why on Halloween night we felt relieved after we had ruined that merchant's front door, painted insults on his windows and dumped more paint on new lumber piled behind his store. We were proud of ourselves when later we saw his White truck driver try to deliver a load of furniture we had ordered to an

* *The New Republic* (February 17, 1968), 15–16. Reprinted by permission of *The New Republic* (© 1968), Harrison-Blaine of New Jersey, Inc.

address in the middle of Big Eleven Lake. "Stupid . . . stupid," one of us said, as the driver stared into the deep water.

If these were the tumultuous feelings of three middle-class, carefully disciplined, northern-bred Negro boys, what extremes are possible when the Negro is poverty-plagued, ghetto-bound, educationally handicapped, self-hating, racially humiliated, frustrated?

After the riots in Negro ghettos during the last three summers, I visited Harlem, Brooklyn, Philadelphia, Cincinnati, Chicago and East St. Louis, talking with people. Listening to their explanations and justifications for the violence, I could see that they—like us three teen-agers in Kansas City—had experienced a badly needed sort of therapy. The rioter *does* gain self-esteem by publicly playing the role of a bold, uncompromising fellow whom others fear. (Example from Philadelphia: "I felt free—'born again'—after I saw what I had done.")

They were rejecting too a Calvinist Doctrine (Predestination), a Protestant Ethic (prayer and hard work solve all problems) and White men's values. Unable to achieve "manhood" and equality in a racially biased value system, the rioter rejects the system as a whole and adopts rules consonant with *his* aspirations. (Chicago: "The White man made the rules and then dealt himself all the aces. To hell with him.")

Symbols of that White power—the police and the exploiting merchants—have to be dishonored, and in the presence of one's peers. (Example from Harlem: "Hell yes, and I'm glad I did it. . . . I cleaned him good. Blue eyes has been robbing and killing us with the law on his side. Got to get rid of him before we can get ourselves straight." Listeners agreed.)

In looting, rioters were taking "part payment" for nearly 250 years of slave labor and a hundred years of discriminatory jobs and wages. (Brooklyn: "I was just taking what belongs to one of my great-grandparents.") (From Philadelphia: "They owe us a hell of a lot more than we took.") Society got the message—and was meant to. (Chicago: "I'm sick of all this crap about violence in the streets. Where I come from a Black son-of-a-bitch ain't safe from the White bastards even at home or in church, let alone the damned streets.") (Harlem: "Yes, we're mad and we want them to know it. We need to burn the whole damned thing down—or blow it up—and get a new start!")

The knowledge that frustration breeds aggression is old and worldwide. The Matsushita Electrical Company of Osaka, Japan, has set up a "human control room" into which an angry or frustrated employee is urged to go, grab a bamboo stick and beat effigies of his bosses until his anger has subsided. The smiling effigies are labeled with the names of supervisors.

We've seen this frustration–aggression pattern again and again in America. When Nat Turner, a half-literate Negro preacher, led seventy-five freedom-seeking slaves in revolt, killing fifty-five Whites, he and sixteen of his followers were executed—following which mobs of Whites took revenge by killing more than a hundred innocent slaves and free Negroes.

In 1863, after President Lincoln had drafted more New York City men for the Union Army, hundreds of white men raged through town, robbing stores and sacking and burning buildings. Many Negroes, including women and children, were beaten to death or hanged to lamp posts. Deaths were estimated at from 400 to 2,000. Eight years later, thirty-three persons were killed during riots of the Irish in New York.

But my concern here is the Black man, whose whole American experience has been dominated by violence. He was enslaved, emancipated, disfranchised, segregated and suppressed—all by violence or the threat of it. For years the lynchings (nearly 4,000 since 1889—principally of Negroes), church bombings, street murders, Klan floggings, and burnings generally went unpunished. No loud outcry welled up over the nation! Not then!

Now some people have the effrontery to wonder why the Black man turns to violence!

# The Separate Worlds of Black, Brown, and White (1967)*

*Piri Thomas*

In the avalanche of testimony made before the United States National Advisory Commission on Civil Disorders, this deposition by Piri Thomas, an author, had great emotional power.

---

* From the testimony of Piri Thomas before the National Advisory Commission on Civil Disorder, September 21, 1967.

You know, Brothers, I have listened, listened real, real nitty-gritty, and as I listened, I asked myself a question, a question that I have asked many times.

Is this America? The land of democracy? Freedom?

I wrote a book called *Down These Mean Streets* and one excerpt in it, I say, "White man, what is your value on skin? . . . Don't you know dark skin is a pride, too?"

I am from a place called a *barrio* in Spanish Harlem where we are for real. These so-called disorders that erupted, you know, in my Spanish Harlem, the barrio, were not just a sort of spontaneous event that come up out of nowhere, just a happening. It was an ugly head of despair, frustration, exploitation, hot- and cold-running cockroaches and king-sized rats, and crummy tenements and slum houses. It was an explosion from a long-burning fuse to a bundle of dynamite that had been slowly burning since I was a kid in East Harlem in the early thirties.

My father is a Black man. My mother is a Puerto Rican woman. And between the two of them, they developed seven sons and one daughter. There are only two sons besides myself—I am the oldest—and my two brothers Ray and Frankie are soldiers for this great America of ours. They hadn't seen each other in a long time, and about a year ago, after a bloody battle in Vietnam, they ran into each other. I wonder what their feelings are.

Puerto Ricans, you—we are supposed to be the "Johnny-come-latelies." We are supposed to be the gentle, inoffensive, happy intelligent, hard-working Puerto Ricans from a little island, smaller than our own Long Island here in New York, and you know, the majority of us suffer from a complex of "me no speaka English" and let me tell you, baby, it was tough because we were surrounded on all sides by different ethnic groups. In most instances we were not welcome because there was so much poverty in Spanish Harlem. Who needed more poor people?

All right. So our fathers and mothers came to a barrio—a barrio is a place—determined to survive by rolling up their sleeves and working when there were jobs available, and then to create a better life for their children.

To give a feeling of this, I would like to read from a play I have written, "Ladies and Misters, What is a Man?"

"Ladies and Misters, Puerto Ricans poured into Nova, New York, their eyes are clogged up with better living days. You understand, of course, that mostly poor Puerto Ricans leave the island, dem dat's got bread come for a tour, take a fast look and make a fast split for the rolling hills of the green islands. But the poor Puerto Ricans, man, they hit the scene like all that jazz of a million plates of rice and beans. Green bananas and codfish is a thing of the past. We are working for so little a day in a factory of sugar cane field ain't no more."

I got a brother that some day I hope to find. In this book his name is Brew. Until the day that I find him again, I'm not going to even tell his real name, but we went down south. I wanted to see what was happening. Oh, yeah, man, forget it.

Brew told me one time. We got real angry at each other, we had a big argument. I tried to dig myself—I figured I should try to get it back on a joke level. What the hell was I trying to put down? Was I trying to tell Brew I was better than he is because he is only Black and I am a Puerto Rican dark-skin? Like those people cut trees at a White man's whim? And whoever heard of a Puerto Rican getting hung? Brew said, "Everybody got some kind of pain going on inside him. I know you're a little————up with some kind of hate called White, that special kind with the no Mister in front of it. Dig it man, say it like it is out loud, like you hate all paddies. Just that————color."

"Brew," I said, bitterly, "just their color. They're damn clean to blast out 'My country 'tis of thee, sweet land of liberty, of thee I sing.'"

And now when I hear it played, I can't help feeling that it is only meant for paddies, Whiteys. It is their national anthem, their sweet land of liberty. "Yeah, I know," Brew said, "Like it says, that all men are created equal with certain deniable rights, if they are not paddies, you know, Whites."

We want to thank you, Mr. Lincoln, Sir. Us blood folks got through that whole Civil War without fear, but we all had one hell of a time still trying to get through that damn Reconstruction.

You know the old saying, "If you're White, that's all right, and if you're Black, that's dead."

I appeared at a hearing on the Bilingual Educational Act. Senator Kennedy invited me. And I read from "Sounds from a Street Kid" of a feeling of what it is to live in a ghetto.

If there is a definite way for a youngster to express himself to an adult—and I am talking about adults, I mean power structure, you people who are here to represent us—I don't think he has yet entirely found it. Even if his speech is articulate, his wants are not. He can only make the basic overtures of asking to be understood.

My own background as a street kid—incidentally, I am an ex-convict, served six years in Comstock, between Sing Sing Prison and Comstock. I'm an ex-drug addict. I am an ex-stickup man. Shot a cop and got shot. In prison I spent the first two years fighting my heart out to keep from being swallowed up by that society. I wrote when I was in prison. I even got my high school diploma and I was very pleased that it didn't say prison diploma. It said "The University of the State of New York."

I spent six years and got out of prison and was re-arrested right at the front gate. But I learned to use my mind. I had said, when I had gotten shot, "If I do not die, my life will be enchantment." Because I come out of a cesspool and I am going to go back there and I'm going to put my arm down there and bring my people up, black, brown, blue, green, multi-colored men.

One thing I ain't got is political affiliations. My only political party is humanity, dignity. I wrote and I said, "I came into this prison a second-class citizen. Now that I'm here I'm supposed to be a third-class citizen. And when they release me someday, I'm going to be a fourth-class citizen."

Later for that, baby. When I get out I'm going to be a first-class citizen because that's my right.

Well, anyway, this a *muchacho* street kid. This is his own language, like he says, nitty-gritty. "Man, like I'm standing here and there ain't nothing happening. Dig it, man, what's in this here world for me, except I gotta give, give, give. I'm tired of being a half-assed nothin', I've come into this stone world of streets, with all its living, laughing, crying and dying. A world full of backyards, roof cops and street sets, all kinds of races of people and acts, of hustlers and rackets, drugs and eyedroppers. A world of those who is and those who ain't."

I'm looking at me and no matter how I set my face, hard rock or soft sullen, I still feel the me inside rumbling low and crazy-like, like I'm mad at something and don't know what it is. Damn it, it's the crap of living every day afraid and not digging what's in tomorrow.

What's the good of living in a present that got no future, no nothin', unless I make something. I fell into this life without no say and I'll be a mother-jumper if I live it without having nothin' to say.

I'm tired of feeling like the invisible cat in the flick, walking all over the place and the only time anybody looks at me is to say, "Get out of the way, kid." I know this world is on a hustle stick and everybody's out to make a buck. This I can dig 'cause it's the same here on the street. I gotta hustle too, and the only way to make it is on a hard kick. I dig that "copping" [getting] is the main bit and "having" is the main rep. You see, I'm really trying to understand and see where the Olders are at.

Right now, I'm standing on my street corner, looking out at your blippy world full of pros, you know, professionals. At all you people what made it a success and be great, a real bunch of killer-dillers. I know about you. I've gone to the big school too. I've dug how to live too. Tell me, do you dig my "royal ass kick"? Are you willing to learn about me and what makes me click? Well, let me run it to you nice and easy.

Could you sense a coming danger, as on a bop you go? Can you feel the bond of belonging when with your boys you go down fighting? A rumbling of bravery, of pure *corazon* [heart] and guts to the *nth* degree? Have you ever punched a guy in the mouth with a garbage can handle? Have you ever spit blood from jammed-up lips? Have you ever felt the pain from a kick in the balls? Have you ever chased in victory in a gang fight supreme or run to tasteless defeat with all the heart you can muster?

Tell me, just tell me, man, did you ever make out in darkened hallways with wet kisses and fumbling hands? Did you ever smother a frightened girl's rejections and force a love from her? Did you ever fill your dreams with magic at what you wanted to be and cursed the bitching mornings for dragging you back on the scene? Did you ever smoke the blast of reefers and lose your freaking mind? Did you ever worry about anything at all, like a feeling of no belonging? Did you ever lover-dubber pass this way?

Did you ever stand on street corners and look the other way, at the world of *muchos ricos* [the very rich] and think, "I ain't got a damn." Did you ever count the garbage that flowed down dirty streets, or dug the backyards who in their glory were a garbage dump's dream? Did you ever stand on rooftops and watch nighttime cover the bad below? Did you ever put your hand around your throat and feel your pulse beat say, "I do belong and there's not gonna be nobody can tell me I'm wrong."

Say, did you ever mess with the hard stuff, cocain, heroin? Did you ever blow pot? Have you ever filled your nose with the wild kick it brought or pushed a hypo, a needle full of the poison, and felt the sharp, dull burning as it ate away your brain? Did you ever feel the down gone high as the drug did take effect? And you felt all your yearnings become sleepy memories and reality become illusion, and you were what you wanted to be?

Did you ever stand small and a little quiet-like and dig your moms and pops fight for lack of money to push off the lack of wants? Did you ever stand with outstretched hands and cop a plea from life and watch your mom's pride on bended knees ask a welfare investigator for the needy welfare check, while you stood there getting from nothing and resenting it just the same? Did you ever feel the thunder of being thrown out for lack of money to pay the rent, or walk in scared darkness, the light bill still unpaid, or cook on canned heat for a bunch of hungry kids, no hiss, no gas—unpaid?

Did you ever sneak into the movies and dig a crazy set where everybody's made it on that wide-wild screen? They ride in long shorts, T-Birds, Continentals, Caddies, and such "viva smoothies," the vines, the clothes like you never ever saw. And oh man, did you ever then go out of that world, and sit on hard stoops and feel such cool hate and ask yourself, "Why man? Why this gotta be for me? The hell with school. I'm going to make that money fast."

I was a kid in Harlem and I had feelings that I wanted to be an architect. I had a Jewish teacher in Harlem High, and I found a book on colleges, and I said, "This is where I want to go you know." So I showed him the college and it was in a place called Georgia. And so the Jewish teacher looked at me, and he was trying to break it to me real nice and easy, like, "Well, you know, Petey, there are some places I can't go and some places that you can't go."

You tell this to a young kid. "What do you mean? I want to study, I want to be somebody." I said, "What do you mean I can't go?" He said, "Well, there is a prejudice, you know." I said, "What is that? I mean, what is that?"

The first time a man called me a nigger I ran and got me a dictionary and found out what nigger meant. Niggardly, stingy. I found out the right term for it and ran right back to him and said, "Hey, *you* are a nigger. *You* are stingy. *You* are niggardly."

I got real angry one time. It was down South and Brew saved my life. We were walking through a White part of town, and a deputy sheriff came out of an alley. And he said, "Where're you goin'?" and I turned around. I said, "I'm going back to my ship," and Brew opened up his mouth and Brew spoke because Brew is from Mobile, Alabama. And he [the deputy sheriff] said, "Oh, you're one of *our* niggers, but *you're* one of them northern niggers." Brew said, "I ain't *nobody's* nigger." And I said, "Me too," and proceeded to beat the living————out of him. I mean it. Because he was going to beat the living————out of us.

You can't put a man up against a wall and expect him to react as a human being. You can't expect people to live in conditions that are abnormal, in ghettos where out in the streets in the summer it is 90 degrees out there and when you crawl back into that hole that you call a home, it is 120 degrees. You can't expect people to live with their hands stretched out. We don't want charity. We want the goddam chance that belongs to all of us. This is our right as human beings.

Every one of you people here have children or grandchildren, and when you go home, they smile and say, "daddy," or "grandpa," or "Grandma." Well, we got them too.

We've got them, too, and when they come up, open up that door, poppy, man, a big smile on my little girl San-Dee's face and my son Ricardo. Well, man, look, we're not asking to take over this country. We're just asking to share it. You give us the name Americans. You preach throughout the whole world democracy. You say this is the land of freedom. "Oh, say can you see."

Yes. "My country 'tis of thee, sweet land of liberty." For whom? For a few? There are Indians starving over there, Navajos, Mexicans that are being treated like dirt, Black men, Brown men, Puerto Ricans, White men.

What is this, the old adage of divide and conquer? Sure. We cut loose from here and some of us, we go back to our ghettos and some of us go back to these beautiful apartments. Look, one of these days all of us are going to make a transition. We are all going to die. From time immemorial we have tried war, and war has not brought anything except the total destruction of mankind, and there is not going to be any more wars now. This is going to be a total distruction, a total hatred.

You think the Civil War was bad? Oh, baby, this is going to be real bad unless White man, Brown man, Black man, Yellow man, get together and really wheel and deal.

I'm going to end up with one thing. I wrote this, and I would like to say it. I call this "Fruits of Dignity."

What is the value of a man's essence of believing
What is the true reality of the cry, "Freedom! Liberty!"
How do I think of these things?
Because within myself, awake or perhaps half-asleep,
As I probe inside of myself, very, very deep.
"Freedom!" The cry heard since the beginning of mankind,
Written on the faces of men's monumental works that
    were created out of faces carved on mountainsides,
Of Pharoah's tombs with diamond and gold-crusted mummies
    laid inside,
The forgotten immortality of sacrifice slaves of millenniums ago,
Who up to this present day we can hear the wailing agonies
Of millions upon millions who left their essence—
Their song of hope and cry of agony and those along the way,
    unto this day.
I am a poet, I am an ex-con,
I am a painter, I am an ex–drug addict.
I am an ex–gang leader, I am a writer,
I am a human being.
Ask me for my positive belief and I will tell you—humanity.
Ask me for my ambition and I will tell you—beauty and
    creativeness.
Ask me what is my golden fleece and I will tell you—harmony
    and the brotherhood of man.
Ask me what is to be my reward and I will tell you—one world.
It is not so simple in a world torn apart by fear
To stand anonymously by the sideline and have your cheap
    sense of victory,
Of either making an unheard of cheer or not an unseen sneer.
I am against the assinine intellectual bore
    as much as I am against the useless, uncreative,
    destructive war.
I have cried and I have tried.
But think not for one moment that I have not been afraid,

Not for the physical fear that death will put his gentle
    hand upon me,
But afraid that I cannot live long enough to see the total
    world forever more free.
Love and understanding, brotherhood and harmony—
Brown man, white man, black man, red man, yellow man,
    multicolored man.
Humanity enjoying the fruits of dignity.
Try well world to make this dream a reality.
Try well, try damn well, or we all soon shall be.
From the present to generations to come—in the
    biblical proverbial hell.
Come on, learn, don't burn.
Reap, don't sleep.
Give—and live.
Share—and care.
To die is very easy.
But it will come at its own time.
Let it be natural—
Not so damn greasy.
When I was a child, I remember—
When I was a young boy, I remember—
When I was a young man, I remember.
Now that I am a man and someday an old man, I will still
    remember—
That there is no conception or interpretation so important
To all mankind than that of—
Fear not—Share—This land belongs to all of us—
One world of chaos—race not to utter destruction,
But rather fly to peace, posterity and the fruitfulness
That is the heart's dream of every human being
No matter where he comes from.
Whether he says "Shalom Aleichem," "Auf Wiedersehen,"
    "Adios," "Bonsoir,"
Whatever the greetings are.
Remember—the smiles on our children's faces are the
    happiness in our hearts—
Their needless deaths in wars uncalled for are the
    anguished tears untold, unheard, in our souls.

We have tried all this hatred, all these fears, all
    these uncertainties,
All these anxieties, all these misunderstandings, all
    these hatreds—genocide.
For all men are brothers.
Tear down the cannons,
Melt down the swords,
Turn the bullets into butterflies,
The bombs into honeybees,
The planes into graceful birds,
The anger into joy,
The hate into love,
The fear into understanding,
And then perhaps one more thing—
We will not be a novalike explosion of our earth,
Disappearing from the face of our unlimited universe.
Come on, world, it is so hard to shake a hand in friendship.
Come on, world, undouble your fists and make it a caressing
    touch of brotherhood instead of Cain killing his brother.
For we all know deep within ourselves
That we would rather live than die,
That we would rather smile than cry,
That we would rather share than not care.
But if you leave us no choice other than to use our voice,
Then we shall become truly a Mars, the God of War,
Rather than Venus, the Goddess of Love.
Every man dies, every man cries.
So therefore why can't every human being take his choice,
For ever after of one world. For ever after.
Harmony, dignity, brotherhood, love—
And a swinging sense of happy laughter.

I would like to end this in one thought. You people, and I am
very glad you invited me, I am very glad to sit here with my brothers,
are the people that have the power. Power is good if you use it for a
positive force. You cannot expect our youngsters, our young people,
to accept what our fathers and forefathers have accepted before.

I would wish, if it were possible, that for three months in the
winter and three months in the summer you would trade places with
us. OK?

So think about that and then come back and see what you do, because I felt very hurt, many of us, when they made big jokes about the rat bill. Real, real angry. And my sister-in-law, who is a very wonderful, gentle woman, said, "I am a good woman in my heart but, I wish that rats would bite their children so they would know how it feels . . . ."

## Police Maltreatment: Bite My Tongue and Keep My Mouth Shut (1965)*

*Wesley R. Brazier*

Police maltreatment does exist in Los Angeles. I have personally been maltreated for minor moving violations on several occasions. I have had the presence of mind to bite my tongue and keep my mouth shut, but you can believe that I boiled inside and felt defenseless.

QUESTION: Could you tell us a few of the several occasions when you have been maltreated?

THE WITNESS: Yes. I can also cite the one that, to me, was even worse in my case, and that was with my wife. And I discussed this one with Deputy Chief Simon, and he went through the record, but my wife couldn't remember the date, so we couldn't find the police officer.

But she was on the way to school at Crenshaw and Vernon, right near the Great Western Savings and Loan. She was making a left turn. She was right behind the police officer on the motorcycle, and as he took off she did too, with the green light, and he went up ahead and stopped another car and then stopped her.

Then she asked the officer, "Why have you stopped me?"

And he said, "You ran the red light."

She said, "Well, officer, I could not have. I was right behind you. You didn't run it and I followed you."

He said, "I said you did. Now, if you want to make something of it, get out of the car and we can settle it right now."

---

* From the testimony of Wesley R. Brazier before the Governor's Commission on the Los Angeles Riots (October 14, 1965), IV, pp. 36–40.

Now, he is a six-foot-two, 200-pound officer, and my little wife is five-feet-two.

Now, had I been there and he said that, you can imagine how I would have felt. I mean, I am defenseless. He is wearing a badge and a pistol and he is a bully.

I have been stopped on numerous occasions, running a light, or failing to yield the right-of-way on a left turn, and I have said, "Officer, I must admit that I violated the law in running this light, my mind was on something else. Would you kindly give me my ticket so I may proceed to an appointment?"

"You are going to listen to what I got to tell you. Now, you know what you could have done? You could have killed somebody." I said, "Officer, I am aware of all this. Would you kindly write me my ticket? I don't need an educational lecture today."

"Oh, you are one of those smart so-and-so's."

I said, "No, I am not————"

JUDGE BROADY: What is "smart so-and-so?"

THE WITNESS: Smart "nigger."

I said, "No, I am not trying to be smart. I merely asked you to give me my ticket."

"If you don't shut up, I will————"

I said, "Officer, if you want to drive me down to the police station, I will go down with you. Give me my ticket or drive me down."

It has been this kind of harassment that I have received where I say it is not so much police brutality as it is police maltreatment, which can incite one into a state where, to defend himself, or to be a man, he doesn't care. And you are going to face more and more of this. The Negro is tired now of being looked down upon and, believe me, he is going to rebel. And when he does, he is going to tackle that policeman.

We have had cases where two women just beat a policeman to death. Two women. Now, they are just sick and tired of this maltreatment.

If we could get Chief Parker to recognize that when criticisms are heaped upon the police department it is not being heaped upon him, and I have said this to the Chief on numerous occasions, that "You are guilty of supporting them by saying that Los Angeles' finest can do no wrong. You have got sadists. You have got egotists. You have got everything on your police department."

And there are not tests developed yet that can pull out the ideal person to be a policeman.

So, I say there is considerable maltreatment. And it is against the Negro, regardless of what his station in life may be. I surely don't go out seeking trouble with the police officers. But, I do feel that I am a taxpayer and I am paying his salary and I think he should learn to respect and talk to me as a taxpayer and as one who is paying his salary.

## I'm Throwing Rocks Because I'm Tired of a White Man Misusing Me (1966)*

Witnesses stated that at this time [the night of August 11–12] young Negro rioters said: "I'm throwing rocks because I'm tired of a White man misusing me." "Man, this is the part of town they have given us, and if they don't want to be killed they had better keep their ——— out of here." "The cops think we are scared of them because they got guns, but you can only die once; if I get a few of them I don't mind dying." "What the hell do you expect me to do? They have been picking on me all my life." "I don't care what you say, I'm going to kick Whitey's ——— tonight." "I wish [Chief of Police] Parker would come out here. I'd like to throw a brick at his ———." "The ——— cops are gone now, but they'll be back and when they do we'll be ready for them. I got a gun like them and if they want to shoot it out it's all right with me."

Sunrise disclosed five burned automobiles amidst a large amount of rubble, broken bricks, stones, and shattered glass in the vicinity of the intersection of Imperial Highway and Avalon Boulevard.

.    .    .    .    .    .    .    .    .    .    .

As an indication of the mood of the crowd of approximately 400 persons who had gathered on Avalon Boulevard near Imperial Highway on Thursday morning, the following comments of youth in the crowd were quoted:

Like why, man, should I go home? These ——— cops have been pushin' me 'round all my life. Kickin' my ——— and things like that. Whitey ain't no good, he talk 'bout law and order, it's his law and his order, it ain't mine. . . .

---

* *The Report of the Governor's Commission on the Los Angeles Riots* (1966), II, pp. 32–33, 43–44, 88–89.

——— , if I've got to die, I ain't dyin' in Vietnam, I'm going to die here. . . .

I don't have no job, I ain't worked for two years — he, the White man, got everything, I ain't got nothin'. What you expect me to do? I get my kicks when I see Whitey running — if they come in here tonight, I'm going to kill me one. . . .

Look, Brother, I ain't scared of them — what they got — a gun? I got one too, and I'm goin' to blast me a cop on that White ——— tonight ——— you'd better believe it. . . .

If them black-and-whites [police cars] come in here tonight — they'd wish they hadn't — we are ready. . . .

I got my stuff [gun] ready, and baby, I mean to use it — I'm going to get me a White ——— tonight — tell them that for me. . . .

They always ——— with the Blood — beatin' them with them sticks, handcuffing women, I saw one of them ——— go up side a cat's head and split it wide open. They treat the Blood like dirt — they been doin' it for years — look how they treated us when we were slaves — we still slaves. . . .

Them White cops are trained to kick niggers ———. I seen too many ——— kickin's to think otherwise. . . .

What I got to do with this country ——— ——— ? ——— Whitey ain't never done a damn thing for Blood except kill us. It's our turn now. . . .

Whitey use his cops to keep us here. We're like hogs in a pen. Then they come in with them silly helmets, sticks and guns and things. Who the ——— Parker think he is — God?

.   .   .   .   .   .   .   .   .   .

At 3:07 A.M. Assemblyman Dymally and Robert Hall informed the L.A.P.D. that several motor vehicles had been overturned and were burning at Compton Avenue and Imperial Highway and at Central Avenue and Imperial. During the time these two men were in the Central Avenue, District Assemblyman Dymally said he observed "young toughs" pulling a Caucasian from an automobile which was stopped for a traffic signal. The youths began to beat the driver and other Negroes at the scene tried to prevent his being injured. The automobile, however, was overturned and burned by the rioters. Police officers handed Assemblyman Dymally a bullhorn and he handed it to Robert Hall who used it to attempt to disperse the mob. At that time the Assemblyman spoke to some of the rioters, saying, "Man, let's cool it," and one of the rioters asked, "Where you from, man? Baldwin Hills?" Dymally said, "No, I live here in Avalon," and the rioter replied, "You must live in some big house." Dymally said, "No, man, I'm the people," and the rioter retorted, "If you're the people, throw it," as he handed the Assemblyman an empty bottle. Dymally replied, "No, man, I'm for peace," and the rioter replied, "No, you're with The Man," referring to the White man.


# The Riot: A Liberating, Identifying Force (1966)*

*Frederick J. Hacker, M.D., with Aljean Harmetz*


Following the 1965 Watts Riot, Governor Edmund G. Brown appointed an eight-member commission, led by a former director of the CIA, John A. McCone, to "investigate the immediate and underlying causes of the Los Angeles riots and to recommend means to prevent their recurrence." The following is from testimony before that commission.

For three years prior to the Watts riot, Dr. Hacker was advisor to the Westminster Neighborhood Association, the largest Negro social welfare agency in Watts.

For the Negroes, what happened in southeastern Los Angeles August [1965] *was* justified legally and morally. Where the police saw Black criminals tearing apart law and order with a cascade of Molotov cocktails, the Negroes of Watts watched freedom fighters liberating themselves with blood and fire. The McCone Report says that only 2 per cent of the Negroes participated in the rioting. It implies that the rest of the Negro community was cowering in darkened houses waiting for the forces of law and order to rescue them. Actually, the majority of the 400,000 Negroes in the area supported the riots. As one high-school girl said afterwards, "Every time I looked out of my window and saw another fire, I felt new joy."

---

* From "What the McCone Commission Didn't See," *Frontier* (March, 1966). Reprinted by permission of *The Nation*.

## Not "Bad" or "Criminal"

The most distinctive generally shared feeling of the Negroes about the riots is that they were not criminal. To some, they were the explosion of a powder keg; to others, a rationally planned demonstration against sustained injustice; to others, a full-scale rebellion; to others, an assertion of racial independence, a kind of racial identity struggle; and for others, a protest against intolerable poverty. For none of the Negroes, however, were the riots "bad" or "criminal" in the sense these words are used by the McCone Commission.

For the Negroes, there was no reason to feel guilt, shame, or regret. Although most of the rioters interviewed believe that it is wrong to "burn," "loot," "break down the law," they felt the looting and burning were merely excesses of a just cause and thus justified. In that respect, the Watts riots were psychologically analagous to the Hungarian Revolution and the Boston Tea Party, where the participants also did not try to excuse the single acts considered "bad" but felt fully justified by their overall cause.

Some psychoanalysts tend to belittle violence as *sickness*. They—like the members of the McCone Commission—ignore the uncomfortable historical evidence that violence can unite, particularly if the violence occurs once and is not repeated. As in the mythology of bullfighting, violence—the ultimate violence that could or does lead to death—is the great unifier, the strange symbol of reality confronted with an ultimate truth. When one is nakedly facing one's destiny, presumably all falsehood and pretense falls away and one is—as described by rioters—"close to God."

## Alternative to Despair

Conventional psychoanalytic theory says that resorting to violence, particularly collective violence, is a regression and a projection of inner feelings of panic and despair. This is undoubtedly true. What is overlooked is that violence is also an effective defense. In other words, violence is an alternative to despair. Through violence, you can rid yourself of a torturing feeling of helplessness and nothingness. Violence makes you feel good—at least for a while. And it could be argued that the "mental health" of the Negro community was much better after the riots than before, because the riots served as a safety valve against the feeling of apathy that was the strongest characteristic of life in Watts.

Life in Watts before the riots was not only deprived. It was dull. Anyone familiar with the psychology of modern crime knows that the search for novelty and the desire to escape monotony is by no means willful, arbitrary, or fanciful. The hunger and search for new experiences—popularly known as "kicks"—indicates just as legitimate a need as the search for food or sexual satisfaction.

The psychological climate of Watts last summer was one of apathy tangled with an acute sense of injustice. The Negroes felt that all the storekeepers were Jews and Italians, who, having suffered exploitation, were out to exploit Negroes. They felt all the policemen assigned to Watts were recent immigrants recruited from the South and therefore sadistic and brutal. Both reactions were serious misconceptions. But most of the carefully collected injustices did result from real deprivation and major suffering, although the suffering was often expressed in trivial terms.

It cost seventy-five cents to cash a check in Watts, while in nearby White communities it cost nothing. Food cost more in Watts. For example, canned peaches cost three cents more than they do in White neighborhood supermarkets. In Watts, there was no promise or possibility of real change. In Watts, there was no "action." In Vietnam people were dying; in Hollywood people were living the sweet life; in Watts nothing ever happened.

To the White Angelenos driving the freeways in their Monzas and Barracudas and Mustangs, Watts was invisible. By an accident of geography, it was underneath the freeway. It was underneath the freeway in the very center of their city, and the White Angelenos roared over it daily without noticing its existence. (Over and over again after the riots, the participants used the same words: "We put ourselves on the map." It was almost as though the riots had been planned as a tourist attraction and the inhabitants were now happy and proud that photographers and curiosity-seekers were descending from the freeways to see where it all took place.)

In Watts, the police often reached for their guns if a Negro approached them even if he only wanted to ask directions. Few cared what happened to Negroes as human beings. To a great extent, only their women could get jobs—usually as servants. The police were continually harassing them—humiliating them by making them spread-eagle over a car hood to be searched, by mimicking their speech, by refusing to call them "Mister" and substituting the insults of "Hey, boy," or "Come here, monkey."

## How Negro Men Saw Themselves

· · · · · · · · · · ·

For the rioters, the riots were fun. The conventional explanation by middle-class parents to their children about sex skips over the important point that sex also can be fun. In much the same way, observers have not understood or have withheld the fact that the riots were fun. There was a carnival in the midst of carnage. Rioters laughed, danced, clapped their hands. Many got drunk. Violence was permissible. Children stayed out all night. Several children between the ages of ten and fourteen (who first asked the permission of their mothers to talk to a White man) later admitted defensively that it was "great fun." ... "It was a little scarey but mostly it was great because everybody had a good time, sort of a ball." ... "Nobody cared if we ever went to bed."

Contrary to the usual pattern of riots, there was hardly any sexual delinquency or increase in sexual activities. Usually rioting, and the uncontrolled, unrestrained, and thus pleasurable descent into repressed and suppressed emotion and the release of all tension in the absence of ordinary inner and outer controls, brings with it sexual promiscuity. But when the lower-class Negro says he "wants to feel like a man," he is talking about status—not sex. The rioters constantly volunteered the information that "we never had to worry about sex." ... "Sex is nothing to get excited about." ... "Whitey makes too much of it." Sex has always been the lower-class Negro's one free pleasure. Homosexual and heterosexual experience starts young. And from the time a boy is ten or eleven, girls are always available. So the release of tension in rioting led not to sexual delinquency, but to looting.

## Mixed Feelings About the Looting

The looting also was fun. There was great glee about the breakdown of a law-enforcement system identified with suppression and injustice. The objects looted from stores were often taken as a symbol of the Mardi Gras atmosphere of liberation from injustice. Some rioters said over and over again that they didn't need the things they stole and could not use them. In many cases, the stolen refrigerators, stoves, television sets and stereo sets were divorced completely from their utilitarian use. They had been coveted for a long time, but after they were stolen, they were often taken apart and abandoned. It was the ultimate in waste, in contempt for the White man's objects—a determined "No" to acculturation, to the White man's world. Rather than useful instruments that had to be guarded and protected and cared for, the looted objects actually became toys.

During the riots there was, to paraphrase Coleridge, "a willing suspension of conscience." In rioting, one loses personal individuality by gaining collective individuality. One "becomes like the others" and this "makes you happy." . . . "I don't think any more." . . . "I had the good feeling that this was right and it was wonderful."

This liberation from conscience and from conscientiousness made possible for the rioters an involvement and an extreme commitment usually denied them. The most important resource the lower-class Negro lacks is the resource to get involved in something or committed to something, including the ordinary values of society that are un-hesitatingly accepted by the middle-class White—and the middle-class Negro-American.

Bayard Rustin says that the Black body has to be used precisely because democratic channels are denied to the Negro, and he has nothing but his body to fight with. During the Watts rioting, the apathy—which is a form of chronic mild depression—was swept away. Real feeling was restored to the Negroes by the full involvement of their bodies and by actual danger. There was ecstatic body involvement. ("It felt good all over." . . . "We were whole again." . . . "We were whole people, not just servants." . . . "We were new.")

Again and again one phrase was repeated: "At last we were where the action was." At last something was happening, and what was happening was extraordinarily important. It was the metamorphosis of the Negroes of southeastern Los Angeles from victims—historical objects—to masters. They were now men. As one explained the change: "It made our males men," and another said, "I saw children respect their fathers for the first time."

## A Shared Feeling of Identity

The people of Watts felt that for those four days they represented all Negroes; the historic plight of the Negroes; all the rebellions against all injustice. They were doing the job that other Negroes were prevented from doing. They were setting an example, starting a pattern. Being able to watch themselves on television screens in store windows, even as they smashed the stores, reinforced their feelings of self-importance. In their simultaneous participation and watching their participation, they felt that the whole nation—Black and White—watched them too. They felt the emotional involvement of the nation in the riot as a symbol. Like lighting the Christmas tree on the White House lawn, it was a shared experience.

There was an extraordinary religious—almost mystical—fervor. Economic and social injustices took on religious meaning. "All God's children got shoes," said one rioter, explaining his looting of a shoe store. The injustices had betrayed the promises of the Bible that all people should be equal and that the lowest is as good as the highest. Watts stood for every deprived Negro community. Frequently there was overt identification with Christ as a sacrificial being who by his suffering takes upon himself and atones for the sins of everybody. But the role of Christ was rejected in the next breath in favor of "being where the action is."

Chapter Six

# Four Major Protest Riots:
# Harlem, Watts, Newark, Detroit

Although the four riots described in this chapter are somewhat different in origin and development—the Detroit riot, for example, witnessed looting by both Blacks and Whites—they are linked together in many several important ways. The most important connection between them is that they are the result of racial suppression and economic repression of the minorities who are the have-nots in society. Kenneth Clark, the eminent psychologist, in his work *Dark Ghetto*, commented on the serious ramifications of this combination of factors in the slum ghetto:

> The poor are always alienated from normal society, and when the poor are Negro, as they increasingly are in the American cities, a double trauma exists—rejection on the basis of class and race is a danger to the stability of the society as a whole. . . . The social dynamics of the dark ghettos can be seen as the restless thrust of a lower-class group to rise into the middle class.*

The shouting in the streets came from the anguished lower non-White classes. Though they expressed themselves in aggressive ways by throwing

---

* Kenneth Clark, *Dark Ghetto* (New York: Harper & Row, 1964), p. 21.

Molotov cocktails, sniping, burning looting and harassing, they acted from wounds suffered in a country which refused to pay them heed—indeed, which refused to recognize their very existence. Addressing a conference, Mayor Robert Wagner of New York likened the poor in the cities to "angry lions":

> There are lions in the streets, angry lions, aggrieved lions, lions who have been caged until the cages crumbled. We had better do something about those lions, and when I speak of lions I do not mean individuals. I mean the spirit of the people. Those who have been neglected and oppressed and discriminated against and misunderstood and forgotten.

Each of the riots described and analyzed in this chapter, is an expression of despair, of an irrepressible statement, of the desire for dignity and for a place in American society. Thus, the rioters struck against the symbols of the status-keepers, namely, the police and White business establishments. It is highly significant that they discriminated in their violent actions, singling out individuals and businesses who had long exploited them.

Another pattern becomes evident in the study of the riots of the sixties. The majority of the middle- and upper-class Americans were unprepared for the retaliation of the urban masses who etiher participated in the riots or who lent support by their actions or words. Hence, the confusion of authority, the needless killing of many innocent persons, the fear and chaos of those untouched by the riots. That contemporary America has had great difficulty in understanding the exercise of new non-White consciousness is suggested by the quick attempt to place the blame on conspirational groups and the political move to establish commissions to investigate the causes of the riots, despite the existence of many solid, albeit unheeded, reports of previous riots.

Many persons who were unaware of the existence of the ghettos were bewildered. To them the minorities in the urban centers were indeed "invisible" men. Freeways, rapid city transit, and expressways brought vehicles swiftly past the ghetto areas; de facto segregation prevented the interracial mingling of children; gerrymandered neighborhoods hindered political contact between ethnic groups; mass media seldom showed minority members except in a context of violence; and history books often ignored them or else treated them in an underhanded, derogatory way.

The riots, then, were a protest against invisibility. Their visible actions can thus be viewed in over 100 riots and especially in the four major riots of the decade: Harlem, Watts, Newark, and Detroit.

# A Nation of Two Societies (1968)*

The enormity of the Detroit Riot in 1967, a city in which Blacks were comparatively better off economically and socially, frightened many persons. Their fears were intensified by the scenes of interracial looting in the city; acts which appeared to border on class war. No longer able to ignore the racial—and now possibly, economic—bitterness in the country, President Johnson appointed a National Advisory Commission on Civil Disorders. Its report, known as the Kerner Report after the head of the Commission, was heralded by many public and academic officials. The Commission pointed to White racism as the main underlying cause of the urban violence and called for a massive program in order to alleviate conditions in the cities, for a re-evaluation of attitudes on the part of Caucasians, and for immediate action. President Johnson ignored the Commission's findings, privately sniped at it, and never carried out its recommendations.

## Introduction

The summer of 1967 again brought racial disorders to American cities, and with them shock, fear and bewilderment to the nation.

The worst came during a two-week period in July, first in Newark and then in Detroit. Each set off a chain reaction in neighboring communities.

On July 28, 1967, the President of the United States established this Commission and directed us to answer three basic questions:

1) What happened?
2) Why did it happen?
3) What can be done to prevent it from happening again?

To respond to these questions, we have undertaken a broad range of studies and investigations. We have visited the riot cities; we have heard many witnesses; we have sought the counsel of experts across the country.

This is our basic conclusion: Our nation is moving toward two societies, one Black, one White—separate and unequal.

Reaction to last summer's disorders has quickened the movement and deepened the division. Discrimination and segregation have long permeated much of American life; they now threaten the future of every American.

---

* From the Report of the United States National Advisory Commission on Civil Disorders (1968), p. 1–11.

This deepening racial division is not inevitable. The movement apart can be reversed. Choice is still possible. Our principal task is to define that choice and to press for a national resolution.

To pursue our present course will involve the continuing polarization of the American community and, ultimately, the destruction of basic democratic values.

The alternative is not blind repression or capitulation to lawlessness. It is the realization of common opportunities for all within a single society.

This alternative will require a commitment to national action—compassionate, massive and sustained, backed by the resources of the most powerful and the richest nation on this earth. From every American it will require new attitudes, new understanding, and, above all, new will.

The vital needs of the nation must be met; hard choices must be made, and, if necessary, new taxes enacted.

Violence cannot build a better society. Disruption and disorder nourish repression, not justice. They strike at the freedom of every citizen. The community cannot—it will not—tolerate coercion and mob rule.

Violence and destruction must be ended—in the streets of the ghetto and in the lives of people.

Segregation and poverty have created in the racial ghetto a destructive environment totally unknown to most White Americans.

What White Americans have never fully understood—but what the Negro can never forget—is that White society is deeply implicated in the ghetto. White institutions created it, White institutions maintain it, and White society condones it.

It is time now to turn with all the purpose at our command to the major unfinished business of this nation. It is time to adopt strategies for action that will produce quick and visible progress. It is time to make good the promises of American democracy to all citizens—urban and rural, White and Black, Spanish-surname, American Indian, and every minority group.

.    .    .    .    .    .    .    .    .    .

## Patterns of Disorder

The "typical" riot did not take place. The disorders of 1967 were unusual, irregular, complex and unpredictable social processes. Like most human events, they did not unfold in an orderly sequence.

However, an analysis of our survey information leads to some conclusions about the riot process.

In general:

> The civil disorders of 1967 involved Negroes acting against local symbols of White American society, authority and property in Negro neighborhoods — rather than against White persons.

> Of 164 disorders reported during the first nine months of 1967, eight (5 per cent) were major in terms of violence and damage; 33 (20 per cent) were serious but not major; 123 (75 per cent) were minor and undoubtedly would not have received national attention as "riots" had the nation not been sensitized by the more serious outbreaks.

> In the 75 disorders studied by a Senate subcommittee, 83 deaths were reported. Eighty-two per cent of the deaths and more than half the injuries occurred in Newark and Detroit. About 10 per cent of the dead and 38 per cent of the injured were public employees, primarily law officers and firemen. The overwhelming majority of the persons killed or injured in all the disorders were Negro civilians.

> Initial damage estimates were greatly exaggerated. In Detroit, newspaper damage estimates at first ranged from $200 million to $500 million; the highest recent estimate is $45 million. In Newark, early estimates ranged from $15 to $25 million. A month later damage was estimated at $10.2 million, over 80 per cent in inventory losses.

. . . . . . . . . .

## Organized Activity

On the basis of all the information collected, the Commission concludes that:

> The urban disorders of the summer of 1967 were not caused by, nor were they the consequence of, any organized plan or "conspiracy."

Specifically, the Commission has found no evidence that all or any of the disorders or the incidents that led to them were planned or directed by any organization or group, international, national or local.

Militant organizations, local and national, and individual agitators, who repeatedly forecast and called for violence, were active in the spring and summer of 1967. We believe that they sought to encourage violence, and that they helped to create an atmosphere that contributed to the outbreak of disorder.

We recognize that the continuation of disorders and the polarization of the races would provide fertile ground for organized exploitation in the future.

Investigations of organized activity are continuing at all levels of government, including committees of Congress. These investigations relate not only to the disorders of 1967 but also to the actions of groups and individuals, particularly in schools and colleges, during this last fall and winter. The Commission has cooperated in these investigations. They should continue.

## The Basic Causes

In addressing the question "Why did it happen?" we shift our focus from the local to the national scene, from the particular events of the summer of 1967 to the factors within the society at large that created a mood of violence among many urban Negroes.

These factors are complex and interacting; they vary significantly in their effect from city to city and from year to year; and the consequences of one disorder, generating new grievances and new demands, become the causes of the next. Thus was created the "thicket of tension, conflicting evidence and extreme opinions" cited by the President.

Despite these complexities, certain fundamental matters are clear. Of these, the most fundamental is the racial attitude and behavior of White Americans toward Black Americans.

Race prejudice has shaped our history decisively; it now threatens to affect our future.

White racism is essentially responsible for the explosive mixture which has been accumulating in our cities since the end of World War II. Among the ingredients of this mixture are:

—*Pervasive discrimination and segregation* in employment, education and housing, which have resulted in the continuing exclusion of great numbers of Negroes from the benefits of economic progress.

—*Black in-migration and White exodus*, which have produced the massive and growing concentrations of impoverished Negroes in our major cities, creating a growing crisis of deteriorating facilities and services and unmet human needs.

—*The Black ghettos* where segregation and poverty converge on the young to destroy opportunity and enforce failure. Crime, drug addiction, dependency on welfare, and bitterness and resentment against society in general and White society in particular are the result.

At the same time, most Whites and some Negroes outside the ghetto have prospered to a degree unparalleled in the history of civilization. Through television and other media, this affluence has been flaunted before the eyes of the Negro poor and the jobless ghetto youth.

Yet these facts alone cannot be said to have caused the disorders. Recently, other powerful ingredients have begun to catalyze the mixture:

—*Frustrated hopes* are the residue of the unfulfilled expectations aroused by the great judicial and legislative victories of the Civil Rights Movement and the dramatic struggle for equal rights in the South.

—*A climate that tends toward approval and encouragement of violence* as a form of protest has been created by White terrorism directed against nonviolent protest; by the open definance of law and federal authority by state and local officials resisting desegregation; and by some protest groups engaging in civil disobedience who turn their backs on nonviolence, go beyond the constitutionally protected rights of petition and free assembly, and resort to violence to attempt to compel alteration of laws and policies with which they disagree.

—*The frustrations of powerlessness* have led some Negroes to the conviction that there is no effective alternative to violence as a means of achieving redress of grievances, and of "moving the system." These frustrations are reflected in alienation and hostility toward the institutions of law and government and the White society which controls them, and in the reach toward racial consciousness and solidarity reflected in the slogan "Black Power."

—*A new mood* has sprung up among Negroes, particularly among the young, in which self-esteem and enhanced racial pride are replacing apathy and submission to "the system."

—*The police are not merely a "spark" factor.* To some Negroes police have come to symbolize White power, White racism and White repression. And the fact is that many police do reflect and express these White attitudes. The atmosphere of hostility and cynicism is reinforced by a widespread belief among Negroes in the existence of police brutality and in a "double standard" or justice and protection— one for Negroes and one for Whites.

To this point, we have attempted to identify the prime components of the "explosive mixture." In the chapters that follow we seek to analyze them in the perspective of history. Their meaning, however, is clear:

In the summer of 1967, we have seen in our cities a chain reaction of racial violence. If we are heedless, none of us shall escape the consequences.

## Harlem: Hatred in the Streets (1964)*

All year—perhaps for all its sixty years—Harlem had been an explosion waiting for a time to go off. Harlem was born with the century, when White New York pushed its Negro problem out of sight, north of 110th Street, and postponed it to another generation. Harlem's people grow up full of anger at the only White men they ever see: the shopkeepers, the rent collectors, the salesmen, the racketeers, and, most of all, the cops—who seem, to Harlem, less a protective force than an occupying army. For months, that anger had smoldered and sputtered; the flash point was near, and almost everyone knew it. First came the rent strikes and the rat protests; then, mounting violence on the subways, and always in the background, like a kind of ritual incantation, the prophecies of the long, hot summer. The knots of jobless, aimless, hopeless men slouched on their tenement stoops in the clinging summer heat with little to do but talk bitterly about "Whitey."

This was the tinder. The spark was struck when an off-duty White police lieutenant named Thomas Gilligan shot and killed a fifteen-year-old Negro boy named James Powell in a sidewalk free-for-all downtown in Yorkville.

There had been sporadic fighting in Yorkville that day, and the police had quelled it without much difficulty because Yorkville is White Man's Territory. But the fuse that was lighted in Yorkville burned quickly to Harlem.

### Litany

Two nights later, CORE workers set up a blue kitchen chair and a miniature American flag at 125th Street and Seventh Avenue—Har-

---

* *Newsweek* (August 3, 1964), 16–20. Copyright Newsweek, Inc. (August, 1964).

lem's main crossroads—and summoned a desultory crowd around for a protest rally. One after another, speakers climbed onto the rickety chair, and more Negroes pressed up to hear their angry litany: "James Powell was shot because he was black . . . It is time to let The Man know that if he does something to us, we are going to do something back. If you say, 'You kick me once, I'm going to kick you twice,' we might get some respect!" And then the crowd marched off to the 123rd Street police station, two blocks away, to demand Lieutenant Gilligan's arrest for murder.

There the crowd grew bigger and uglier; it hooted, "Killer cops! Murderers!" The police tried to seal off the block. There was a scuffle; two-dozen marchers and cops went down in a heap. "That's it!" a police inspector cried. "Lock 'em up!" Officers hustled sixteen demonstrators inside and started bulling the others down the street.

### We Are Home

Almost in a matter of minutes Central Harlem was aflame with hatred—that night and the next and the next. Rioters raged madly through the streets, scattering as police counterattacked, regrouping to charge again. Rocks, bricks, and garbage-can lids rained down on the cops. Bottles looped down from tenement rooftops, popping on the pavement. Molotov cocktails burst in sheets of flame five feet high. Trash cans were set afire. One blaze broke out in a movie theater on Seventh Avenue, another in the National Memorial African Bookstore on Seventh Avenue—a militant nationalist hangout ornamented with a picture of a black Jesus and a sign that says, "God Dam White Man." All along 125th and Seventh and Lenox, Harlem's main business streets, looters—some in organized gangs—smashed store windows, climbed inside, and crawled out with armloads of trophies: food, clothing, shoes, jewelry, radios—and rifles. Facing a swarm of rioters one night, a sweating, red-faced police captain pleaded into a bullhorn: "Go home! Go home!" and a voice came back, shrill, taunting: "We *are* home, baby!"

The police fought back with main force—with billies and bullets. Reinforcements and off-duty volunteers streamed in from all five boroughs, sealing off the 57-block heart of Central Harlem and flooding the streets with as many as 400 helmeted cops. Buses brought New York's crack, riot-trained commando unit, the Tactical Patrol Force. Again and again, wherever a menacing crowd gathered, the cry went up—"Charge!"—and police waded in, clubbing rioters, rooters, and sometimes bystanders alike with their night sticks. When clubs didn't halt the rain of missiles, the cops crouched behind cars and lampposts for cover and sent crackling volleys of revolver fire into the air—or just above the rooftop line where the bottled bombers lurked beneath the skyline.

## Gunsmoke

But every bullet and every bloodied head was a new incitement; the show of force spawned its own fast-spreading atrocity rumors. Negro leaders charged that cops were clubbing Negroes indiscriminately—even those who tried to help the injured to hospitals or to a first-aid station at CORE's 125 Street headquarters. They also accused the police of shooting to kill—not just to scare the rioters. The statistics hardly bore out the charge: a dozen reported gunshot wounds among the countless thousands of rounds fired. But one rioter—a hard-case ex-convict who had been tossing bricks from a tenement roof—was struck in the forehead and killed. And a twenty-three-year-old woman charged she was trying to find her way through the crowds to a taxi when a policeman aimed his revolver at her and fired five times, wounding her once in the leg. "I remember screaming at him, 'You shot me! You shot me!' " she said. "He looked at me and said, 'Well, lay down and die then.' "

The ugly scenes spread. Melvin Drummond—a twenty-four-year-old entertainer just back from a Peace Corps tour of Europe—said he was clubbed, handcuffed, clubbed again, and arrested as he came out of a Harlem subway station. Other cops broke into Sam's West Side Bar and Grill at Eighth and 131st Street in pursuit of a band of bottle tossers. Negroes streamed out, blood spilling down their shirt fronts, screaming into the night: "This cop, he brutalizes my arm . . . . Put this on TV, put this on TV! I want the world to see this!"

## "They Got One"

Sidewalks were littered with glass and splotched with blood; the injured sprawled in doorways, friends poking cigarettes between their puffed lips. A drunken Negro woman lay down in the middle of Seventh Avenue in her own private, pixillated demonstration. But, in the hysteria, rumors swept the crowd to new anger: "Did you see that? They shot that woman down in cold blood . . . Women and children, beating up women and children . . . They're just trying to pick us off one by one." Another knot clustered at the Harlem Hospital emergency entrance, watching the wounded come in, cursing the cops: "Butchers! Rotten butcher bastards! You proud of yourself, White man?" A White man was carried past on a stretcher. "He's White, he's White!" someone whooped. "That's good! They got one!"

Responsible Negro leaders worked desperately to restore order. But they were badly hampered by a series of deliberate incitements to further rioting by Black nationalist leaders and Communist agitprop specialists. And sometimes their own anger so overwhelmed them that their calls for order seemed to add new fuel to the fire in the streets.

### "Blood Bath"

CORE national director James Farmer spent his nights in Harlem pleading for order and his days trying to negotiate concessions from City Hall. But, on TV and in newspaper interviews, he bitterly repeated the very atrocity rumors that had so fired the rioters—and, by repeating them, gave them wider circulation. "I saw a blood bath," he cried. "I saw with my own eyes violence, a bloody orgy of police . . . ." Police heatedly denied it and called Farmer's words inflammatory.

Still, Farmer did argue for a return to law and order, and so did the other established leaders. Vacationing in Wyoming, NAACP executive secretary Roy Wilkins sent back word: "I don't care how angry the Negroes are . . . We can't leave [our cause] to the bottle droppers and rock throwers." Courtly old A. Philip Randolph, Negro labor-union leader and a Harlemite for fifty of his seventy-five years, warned that violence "could elect Senator Goldwater . . . which would be the greatest disaster to befall Negroes since slavery." And Harlem's own leadership —hopelessly splintered in the past—found itself drawn together in the quest for peace.

But the flames had raged out of control; the established leaders found themselves only anguished spectators at the battle, their peace appeals unheeded. Late in the week, Wilkins called a summit conference of the nation's top Negro leaders in New York for this week to talk about Harlem and its unsettling political implications—a mission important enough to summon Martin Luther King from the racial battlegrounds of the South. The mission: striking a balance between protest action and political discretion. "The promise of The Civil Rights Act of 1964 could well be diminished or nullified," Wilkins said, "and a decade of increasingly violent and futile disorder ushered in if we do not play our hand coolly and intelligently."

## Guerrilla War

But what happened already in Harlem was not to be undone by reasoned words; the maddened rioters seemed to hear only the voices of anger. At a church rally, Bayard Rustin, the angular intellectual who organized last year's March on Washington, called for volunteer street patrols to try to talk the menacing crowds into going home. He was hooted down. But Jesse Gray, the firebrand Harlem rent-strike leader, drew cheers when he cried out for "guerrilla warfare" and for "100 skilled Black revolutionaries who are ready to die!" Rustin got seventy-five volunteers. Gray claimed eighty-five.

Young James Powell's funeral was held that night, and a milling, menacing crowd of 1,000 drew up in the streets outside the Levy and Delany Funeral Home at Seventh Avenue and 132nd Street. "Though I walk through the valley of the shadow of death . . ." the preacher intoned; his words were lost in a fresh fusillade of bottles and a new crackle of gunfire outside. As Powell's weeping mother was helped into a car, Rustin climbed into a sound truck. "I urge you to go home," he said. "The thing we need to do most is respect this woman whose son was shot." But the crowd hooted: "Uncle Tom! Uncle Tom!"

"I'm prepared to be a Tom," Rustin said evenly, "if it's the only way I can save women and children from being shot down in the street. And if you're not willing to do the same, you're fools."

There was a new round of boos and a fresh chant: "We want Malcolm X! We want Malcolm X!"* And Bayard Rustin, a 23-arrest veteran of the struggle for Negro equality, stepped sadly down to help a bloodied Negro to a hospital. He was back next night, locking arms with Farmer to lead a line of 150 angry youths off the 125th Street battleground toward their homes. But cops sent up flares to light the block; some Negroes pitched some pop bottles; the police returned a fresh salvo of warning shots; the peace march atomized into dashing, howling, marauding bands.

For the Farmers and the Rustins, the tragic fact was that Harlem was deeply and desperately beyond the reach of the established leaders in their downtown offices—and they knew it. Rustin shared Harlem's anger. Late in the week, he journeyed South to Jackson, Mississippi, for an emotional, arm-waving speech to a civil-rights rally: "For years, people have come to New York from Mississippi to tell us what racial

---

* Malcolm X was a former top aide of Elijah Muhammed, leader of the Black Muslims. Later he broke with the movement and was assassinated in 1965.

hell is like. Now I reverse the process." And he understood Harlem's alienation. "I have nothing but sympathy for their booing Farmer and me," he told *Newsweek's* Pat Reilly. "It educates me. Neither of us deals daily with their problems . . . The people now say, 'We want Farmer and Rustin to get off their behinds and produce results.' "

But this time the leadership could not produce the results Harlem wanted.

. . . . . . . . . .

## New Riots

Harlem was quiet that night; it seemed merely to have spluttered down, from riotous fury to random violence and looting by roaming teen-agers, then finally to a kind of unsettled armistice. But the riots were not over; they had only shifted ground, across the East River, to the tumble-down Bedford-Stuyvesant section of Brooklyn.

Here again the trouble began when CORE called a rally at Fulton Street and Nostrand Avenue to try to contain the nascent fury. But the rally dissolved into a burst of bottle-tossing and show-window smashing up and down the Nostrand shopping district.

The next night, as leftist and Black nationalist orators were haranguing a curbside crowd of 1,000, some teen-agers idling on the fringes smashed a store window. The crowd scattered, then straggled back and regrouped. Someone set off a string of firecrackers. The reports crackled like gunfire; the police drew their revolvers and fired warning shots into the air.

That night and the next, rioters and looters milled through Bedford-Stuyvesant. Mounted police charged the rioters, billies swinging like cavalry sabers. Glass crunched underfoot. The pillagers passed stolen goods hand to hand out of store windows, leaving behind a litter of abandoned loot and a tangle of metal screens dangling crazily from store windows out onto the sidewalks. One Negro grocer had hung out a hand-lettered sign: "This is a Black store." But nobody cared; the window was smashed, the store rifled with the rest. Some 400 stores were sacked by the marauders those two nights. Two looters caught in the act were critically wounded by police gunfire.

Throughout the week, as the riots swirled and eddied through the streets of Harlem and Brooklyn, Negro leaders worked unceasingly to get their message through to the mob. "Cool it, baby," pleaded one NAACP leaflet in the ghetto's own argot, "the message has been delivered . . . . Folks like Senator Goldwater, Governor Wallace of Alabama, the John Birchers, and extremists are fixing to do us up, and if we don't play it smart, we'll give them the excuse they've been looking for."

## Cease-fire

Now and again, the "White backlash" flicked out, menacingly. At New York police headquarters, on Manhattan's Centre Street, CORE workers set up a picket line to press their demands for the civilian review board and to protest alleged police brutality. The neighborhood is heavily Italian, and White teen-agers shelled the picket line with rotten eggs and rocks, injuring several cops. "Go back to Harlem!'" they hooted. "Communists! Goldwater for President!"

Then, gradually, a tentative cease-fire settled in. Here and there in Harlem and Brooklyn, sporadic outbreaks continued, and the cops patroling the ghetto streets still wore tin hats. But the humid summer nights turned suddenly cool, and tempers seemed to subside with the temperature. Now there was time to measure the damage in this explosion: one dead, 141 (including 48 cops) seriously injured, 519 arrests, and property losses in the hundreds of thousands of dollars. And now there was time to think about what might be done to keep Harlem and Bedford-Stuyvesant from exploding again.

There were some beguilingly easy answers. One was that the hardcore rioters were not rebels but thieves, that the tempers raised by the Powell case were only a convenient cover for pilferage. And indeed, Harlem was aswarm, by day, with small-businessmen hawking the loot that Harlem had yielded by night. Outside Sugar Ray's Cafe at 122nd Street and Seventh Avenue, in full view of the helmeted police patrols, a man opened the trunk of a gray Chevvy and shouted: "We got shoes, dresses, suits, beer, jewelry, an' even a few cans of tomato juice." A few passers-by stopped and bought—men's suits for $10, shoes for $5 a pair, beer for a nickel a king-size can. Finally, cops shooed the peddler away. "Damn," he grunted. "Things gettin' so bad in Harlem you can't make an honest living any more."

## Extremists

It was easy, too, to blame the extremists—and especially the Communists—who had done their best to stoke the flames of riot still higher. "I am a Communist," said William Epton, chairman of the Harlem Progressive Labor Club. "Since the rioting . . . we've had maybe 300 volunteers. We'll work with any group in Harlem, Black Nationalists, Muslims, or anybody else where we agree on issues." Even as the fires were dying, the Harlem Defense Council—which shares Lenox Avenue offices with Epton's group—circulated posters with a mug shot of Lieutenant Gilligan headed WANTED FOR MURDER. And police caught a seventeen-year-old boy handing out crude, unsigned mimeographed leaflets with a recipe for Molotov cocktails: "[Take] any bottle . . . Fill with gasoline . . . Use rag as wick . . . Light rag . . . Toss and see them run!"

On the afternoon of the fourth day, Acting Mayor Screvane said the disorders were incited in part by "fringe groups, including the Communist Party"; he thought the FBI should look into where they got their money—and why they made such "inflammatory . . . anti-American . . . statements."

## Grievances

But neither answer was adequate. The explosion was as old as Harlem, as wide-ranging as all the grievances that Harlem harbors, as sharp as the bitterness with which Harlem looks out on the twinkling lights and the towering spires of Whitey's world downtown. Harlem's unemployment rate is double the white man's; one Negro man in four is out of work, and the average Negro family earns $3,480 a year to the city-wide average of $5,103. Families splinter; only half of Central Harlem's children live with both parents. Kids lag behind in their segregated ghetto schools, and more than half who enter high school drop out. Harlem's homes are too often rundown and rat infested and overcrowded—a quarter-million people jammed into $3\frac{1}{2}$ square miles. But Harlem's mostly absentee landlords get $50 to $74 a month for a one-room flat that would rent for $30 to $49 in a White slum.

And Harlem is full of free-floating anger. Its homicide rate is six times New York's, its juvenile delinquency twice as high, its narcotics rate ten times as high. On any steaming summer Saturday, Nationalists commandeer the corners along gaudy, brassy 125th Street to preach hatred of Whitey, Charlie, The Man, the blue-eyed devil downtown. And there are always people to listen. In a recent study, Harlem Youth Opportunities Unlimited, Inc. (HARYOU)—one of two social agencies managing a massive, $110 million self-help program only now getting under way—called Harlem a "powerless colony," run economically, politically, and socially by white New York. And James Baldwin, its emigré writer, called it a cage. In his Harlem years, he said, "I hated and feared White people. This didn't mean that I loved Black people; on the contrary, I despised them, and the ghetto from which they could never escape. In effect, I hated and feared the world."

The White cop, for much of Black Harlem, is only Whitey's enforcer, bully-boy, sentry, and pawn—and the riot settled nothing. "The real criminal in Harlem," a Harlem housewife in pedal-pushers told *Newsweek's* Claude Lewis, "is the cops. They permit dope, numbers, whores, gangsters to operate here, and all the time they get money under the table—and I ain't talkin' about $2 neither." On 125th Street, a helmeted policeman walked down the white line in the roadway. "Look at that sonuvabitch," a Negro youth muttered. A car zipped by, narrowly missing the officer. "If I was driving," the boy said, "I'd run him into the goddam river."

And the cops were the symbol for all of Harlem's formless bitterness. "They've been playing Russian roulette with us for years," Kenneth Clark, the Negro psychologist, said angrily. "What disgusts me is the pretense of shock, surprise, horror. The horrible living conditions, the sanitation, pushing people around—apparently nobody gives a damn about it. They send hundreds and hundreds and thousands of cops. They would do better to send one-third as many building inspectors or a thousand sanitation workers, or just an attempt at proper schooling. . . . But you know what I think we're going to get? 'Quiet the natives, then go on with business as usual.' "

### The Choice

That was New York's choice to make. The riots last week were neither the first nor the worst in Harlem's dark history; there had been others, in 1935 and in 1943, and all the citizens committees they spawned hadn't really changed Harlem. But this time the riots were part of the chain of events called the Negro Revolt, and they would not be so easily forgotten. On 128th Street last week, a balding barber stood in his shop and mused: "Course now, I ain't saying I *like* what these kids are doin', but I don't *dis*like it either. They gettin' more action than the politicians, the speechmakers on the corners, the social workers, and all the rest of 'em put together." He paused and puffed his cigar. "When you think about it," he said, "this thing is awful. But nobody ever thinks about Harlem until something like this happens."

# The Watts Manifesto (1965)*

*Bayard Rustin*

Bayard Rustin is perhaps best known for his work as organizer and co-ordinator of the historic March on Washington in 1963. Mr. Rustin was formerly the field secretary of CORE, and has since contributed his organizational talents to numerous civil-rights movements.

The riots in the Watts section of Los Angeles last August continued for six days, during which 34 persons were killed, 1,032 were injured, and some 3,952 were arrested. Viewed by many of the rioters themselves as their "manifesto," the uprising of the Watts Negroes brought out in the open, as no other aspect of the Negro protest has done, the despair and hatred that continue to brew in the northern ghettoes despite the civil-rights legislation of recent years and the advent of the "War on Poverty." With national attention focused on Los Angeles, Governor [Edmund G.] Brown created a commission of prominent local citizens, headed by John A. McCone, to investigate the causes of the riots and to prescribe remedies against any such outbreaks in the future. Just as the violent confrontation on the burning streets of Watts told us much about the underlying realities of race and class relations in America—summed up best, perhaps, by the words of Los Angeles Police Chief William Parker, "We're on top and they're on the bottom" —so does the McCone Report, published under the title *Violence in the City—An End or a Beginning?*, tell us much about the response of our political and economic institutions to the Watts "manifesto."

Like the much-discussed Moynihan Report, the McCone Report is a bold departure from the standard government paper on social problems. It goes beyond the mere recital of statistics to discuss, somewhat sympathetically, the real problems of the Watts community— problems like unemployment, inadequate schools, dilapidated housing— and it seems at first glance to be leading toward constructive programs. It never reaches them, however, for, again like the Moynihan Report, it is ambivalent about the basic reforms that are needed to solve these

---

* From "The Watts 'Manifesto' and the McCone Report," *Commentary* (March, 1966), 29–35. Reprinted from *Commentary*, by permission, copyright © 1966 by the American Jewish Committee.

problems and therefore shies away from spelling them out too explicity. Thus, while it calls for the creation of 50,000 new jobs to compensate for the "spiral of failure" that it finds among the Watts Negroes, the McCone Report does not tell us how these jobs are to be created or obtained and instead recommends existing programs which have already shown themselves to be inadequate. The Moynihan Report, similarly, by emphasizing the breakdown of the Negro family, also steers clear of confronting the thorny issues of Negro unemployment as such.

By appearing to provide new viewpoints and fresh initiatives while at the same time repeating, if in more sophisticated and compassionate terms, the standard White stereotypes and shibboleths about Negroes, the two reports have become controversial on both sides of the Negro question. On the one hand, civil-rights leaders can point to the recognition in these reports of the need for jobs and training, and for other economic and social programs to aid the Negro family, while conservatives can find confirmed in their pages the Negro penchant for violence, the excessive agitation against law and order by the Civil Rights Movement, or the high rates of crime and illegitimacy in the Negro community; on the other hand, both sides have criticized the reports for feeding ammunition to the opposition. Unfortunately, but inevitably, the emphasis on *Negro* behavior in both reports has stirred up an abstract debate over the interpretation of data rather than suggesting programs for dealing with the existing and very concrete situation in which American Negroes find themselves. For example, neither report is concerned about segregation and both tacitly assume that the Civil Rights Acts of 1964 and 1965 are already destroying this system. In the case of the McCone Report, this leaves the writers free to discuss the problems of Negro housing, education, and unemployment in great detail without attacking the conditions of de facto segregation that underlie them.

The errors and misconceptions of the McCone Report are particularly revealing because it purports to deal with the realities of the Watts riots rather than with the abstractions of the Negro family. The first distortion of these realities occurs in the opening chapter—"The Crisis: An Overview"— where, after briefly discussing the looting and beatings, the writers conclude that "The rioters seem to have been caught up in an insensate rage of destruction." Such an image may reflect the fear of the White community that Watts had run amok during six days in August, but it does not accurately describe the major motive and mood of the riots, as subsequent data in the report itself indicate. While it is true that Negroes in the past have often turned the violence inflicted on them by society in upon themselves—"insensate rage" would perhaps have been an appropriate phrase for the third day of the 1964 Harlem riots—the whole point of the outbreak in Watts was that it marked the first major rebellion of Negroes against their own masochism and was carried on with the express purpose of asserting that they would no longer quietly submit to the deprivation of slum life.

This message came home to me over and over again when I talked with the young people in Watts during and after the riots, as it will have come home to those who watched the various television documentaries in which Negroes of the community were permitted to speak for themselves. At a street-corner meeting in Watts when the riots were over, an unemployed youth of about twenty said to me, "We won." I asked him: "How have you won? Homes have been destroyed, Negroes are lying dead in the streets, the stores from which you buy food and clothes are destroyed, and people are bringing you relief." His reply was significant: "We won because we made the whole world pay attention to us. The police chief never came here before; the mayor always stayed uptown. We made them come." Clearly it was no accident that the riots proceeded along an almost direct path to City Hall.

Nor was the violence along the way random and "insensate." Wherever, a storeowner identified himself as a "poor working Negro trying to make a business" or as a "Blood Brother," the mob passed the store by. It even spared a few White businesses that allowed credit or time purchases, and it made a point of looting and destroying stores that were notorious for their high prices and hostile manners. The McCone Report itself observes that "the rioters concentrated on food markets, liquor stores, clothing stores, department stores and pawn shops." The authors "note with interest that no residences were deliberately burned, that damage to schools, libraries, public buildings was minimal and that certain types of business establishments, notably service stations and automobile dealers, were for the most part unharmed." It is also worth noting that the rioters were much more inclined to destroy the stock of the liquor stores they broke into than to steal it, and according to the McCone Report, "there is no evidence that the rioters made any attempt to steal narcotics from pharmacies . . . which were looted and burned."

This is hardly a description of a Negro community that has run amok. The largest number of arrests were for looting—not for arson or shooting. Most of the people involved were not habitual thieves; they were members of a deprived group who seized a chance to possess things that all the dinning affluence of Los Angeles had never given them. There were innumerable touching examples of this behavior. One married couple in their sixties was seen carrying a couch to their home, and when its weight became too much for them, they sat down and rested on it until they could pick it up again. Langston Hughes tells of another woman who was dragging a sofa through the streets and who stopped at each interesction and waited for the traffic light to turn green. A third woman went out with her children to get a kitchen set, and after bringing it home, she discovered they needed one more chair in order to feed the whole family together; they went back to get the chair and all of them were arrested.

If the McCone Report misses the point of the Watts riots, it shows even less understanding of their causes. To place these in perspective, the authors begin by reviewing the various outbursts in the Negro ghettoes since the summer of 1964 and quickly come up with the following explanations: "Not enough jobs to go around, and within this scarcity not enough by a wide margin of a character which the untrained Negro could fill. . . . Not enough schooling to meet the special needs of the disadvantaged Negro child whose environment from infancy onward places him under a serious handicap." Finally, "a resentment, even hatred, of the police as a symbol of authority."

For the members of the special Commission these are the fundamental causes of the current Negro plight and protest, which are glibly summed up in the ensuing paragraph by the statement that "Many Negroes moved to the city in the last generation and are totally unprepared to meet the conditions of city life." I shall be discussing these "causes" in detail as we go along, but it should be noted here that the burden of responsibility has already been placed on these hapless migrants to the cities. There is not one word about the conditions, economic as well as social, that have pushed Negroes out of the rural areas; nor is there one word about whether the cities have been willing and able to meet the demand for jobs, adequate housing, proper schools. After all, one could as well say that it is the *cities* which have been "totally unprepared" to meet the "conditions of *Negro* life," but the moralistic bias of the McCone Report, involving as it does an emphasis on the decisions of men rather than the pressure of social forces, continually operates in the other direction.

The same failure of awareness is evident in the Report's description of the Los Angeles situation (the Negro areas of Los Angeles "are not urban gems, neither are they slums," the Negro population "has exploded," etc.). The authors do concede that the Los Angeles transportation system is the "least adequate of any major city," but even here they fail to draw the full consequences of their findings. Good, cheap transportation is essential to a segregated working-class population in a big city. In Los Angeles a domestic worker, for example, must spend about $1.50 and one and a half to two hours to get to a job that pays $6 or $7 a day. This both discourages efforts to find work and exacerbates the feeling of isolation.

A neighborhood such as Watts may seem beautiful when compared to much of Harlem (which, in turn, is an improvement over the Negro section of Mobile, Alabama)— but it is still a ghetto. The housing is run-down, public services are inferior, the listless penned-in atmosphere of segregation is oppressive. Absentee landlords are the rule, and most of the businesses are owned by Whites: neglect and exploitation reign by day, and at night, as one Watts Negro tersely put it, "There's just the cops and us."

The McCone Report, significantly, also ignores the political atmosphere of Los Angeles. It refers, for example, to the repeal in 1964 of the Rumford Act—the California fair-housing law—in these words: "In addition, many Negroes here felt and were encouraged to feel that they had been affronted by the passage of Proposition 14." Affronted, indeed! The largest state in the Union, by a three-to-one majority, abolishes one of its own laws against discrimination and Negroes are described as regarding this as they might the failure of a friend to keep an engagement. What they did feel—and without any need of encouragement—was that while the rest of the North was passing civil-rights laws and improving opportunities for Negroes, their own state and city were rushing to reinforce the barriers against them.

The McCone Report goes on to mention two other "aggravating events in the twelve months prior to the riot." One was the failure of the poverty program to "live up to [its] press notices," combined with reports of "controversy and bickering" in Los Angeles over administering the program. The second "aggravating event" is summed up by the report in these words:

> Throughout the nation unpunished violence and disobedience to law were widely reported, and almost daily there were exhortations here and elsewhere, to take the most extreme and illegal remedies to right a wide variety of wrongs, real and supposed.

It would be hard to frame a more insidiously equivocal statement of the Negro grievance concerning law enforcement during a period that included the release of the suspects in the murder of the three civil-rights workers in Mississippi, the failure to obtain convictions against the suspected murders of Medgar Evers and Mrs. Violet Liuzzo, the Gilligan incident in New York, the murder of Reverend James Reeb, and the police violence in Selma, Alabama—to mention only a few of the more notorious cases. And surely it would have been more to the point to mention that throughout the nation Negro demonstrations have almost invariably been nonviolent, and that the major influence on the Negro community of the Civil Rights Movement has been the strategy of discipline and dignity. Obsessed by the few prophets of violent resistance, the McCone Commission ignores the fact that never before has an American group sent so many people to jail or been so severely punished for trying to uphold the law of the land.

It is not stretching things too far to find a connection between these matters and the treatment of the controversy concerning the role of the Los Angeles police. The report goes into this question at great length, finally giving no credence to the charge that the police may have contributed to the spread of the riots through the use of excessive force. Yet this conclusion is arrived at not from the point of view of the Watts Negroes, but from that of the city officials and the police. Thus, the report informs us, in judicial hearings that were held on thirty-two of the thirty-five deaths which occurred, twenty-six were ruled justifiable homicides, but the Report—which includes such details as the precise time Mayor Yorty called Police Chief Parker and when exactly the National Guard was summoned—never tells us what a "justifiable homicide" is considered to be. It tells us that "of the thirty-five killed, one was a fireman, one was a deputy sheriff, and one was a Long Beach policeman," but it does not tell us how many Negroes were killed or injured by police or National Guardsmen. (Harry Fleischman of the American Jewish Committee reports that the fireman was killed by a falling wall; the deputy sheriff, by another sheriff's bullet; and the policeman, by another policeman's bullet.) We learn that of the 1,032 people reported injured, ninety were police officers, thirty-six were firemen, ten were National Guardsmen, twenty-three were from government agencies. To find out that about 85 per cent of the injured were Negroes, we have to do our own arithmetic. The Report contains no information as to how many of these were victims of police force, but one can surmise from the general pattern of the riots that few could have been victims of Negro violence.

The Report gives credence to Chief Parker's assertion that the rioters were the "criminal element in Watts" yet informs us that of the 3,438 adults arrested, 1,164 had only minor criminal records and 1,232 had never been arrested before. Moreover, such statistics are always misleading. Most Negroes, at one time or another, have been picked up and placed in jail. I myself have been arrested twice in Harlem on charges that had no basis in fact: once for trying to stop a police officer from arresting the wrong man; the second time for asking an officer who was throwing several young men into a paddy wagon what they had done. Both times I was charged with interfering with an arrest and kept overnight in jail until the judge recognized me and dismissed the charges. Most Negroes are not fortunate enough to be recognized by judges.

.    .    .    .    .    .    .    .    .    .

Certainly these were "aggravating factors" that the McCone Report should properly have mentioned. But what is more important to understand is that even if every policeman in every Black ghetto behaved like an angel and were trained in the most progressive of police academies, the conflict would still exist. This is so because the ghetto is a place where Negroes do not want to be and are fighting to get out of. When someone with a billy club and a gun tells you to behave yourself amid these terrible circumstances, he becomes a zoo keeper, demanding of you, as one of "these monkeys" (to use Chief Parker's phrase), that you accept abhorrent conditions. He is brutalizing you by insisting that you tolerate what you cannot, and ought not, tolerate.

In its blithe ignorance of such feelings, the McCone Report offers as one of its principal suggestions that speakers be sent to Negro schools to teach the students that the police are their friends and that their interests are best served by respect for law and order. Such public-relations gimmicks, of course, are futile—it is hardly a lack of contact with the police that creates the problem. Nor, as I have suggested, is it only a matter of prejudice. The fact is that when Negroes are deprived of work, they resort to selling numbers, women, or dope to earn a living; they must gamble and work in poolrooms. And when the policeman upholds the law, he is depriving them of their livelihood. A clever criminal in the Negro ghettoes is not unlike a clever "operator" in the White business world, and so long as Negroes are denied legitimate opportunities, no exhortations to obey the rules of the society and to regard the police as friends will have any effect.

.    .    .    .    .    .    .    .    .    .

The Watts manifesto is a response to realities that the McCone Report is barely beginning to grasp. Like the liberal consensus which it embodies and reflects, the Commission's imagination and political intelligence appear paralyzed by the hard facts of Negro deprivation it has unearthed, and it lacks the political will to demand that the vast resources of contemporary America be used to build a genuinely great society that will finally put an end to these deprivations. And what is most impractical and incredible of all is that we may very well teach impoverished, segregated, and ignored Negroes that the only way they can get the ear of America is to rise up in violence.


# Newark: On the Salt Marshes of the Passaic River (1968)*

Founded in 1666, the city, part of the Greater New York City port complex, rises from the salt marshes of the Passaic River. Although in 1967 Newark's population of 400,000 still ranked it thirtieth among American municipalities, for the past twenty years the White middle class had been deserting the city for the suburbs.

In the late 1950's the desertions had become a rout. Between 1960 and 1967, the city lost a net total of more than 70,000 White residents. Replacing them in vast areas of dilapidated housing where living conditions, according to a prominent member of the County Bar Association, were so bad that "people would be kinder to their pets," were Negro migrants, Cubans and Puerto Ricans. In six years the city switched from 65 per cent white to 52 per cent Negro and 10 per cent Puerto Rican and Cuban.

The White population, nevertheless, retained political control of the city. On both the City Council and the Board of Education seven

---

* From the *Report of the United States National Advisory Commission on Civil Disorders* (1968), pp. 57–67.

of nine members were White. On other key boards the disparity was equal or greater. In the Central Ward, where the medical college controversy raged, the Negro constitutents and their White councilman found themselves on opposite sides of almost every crucial issue.

The municipal administration lacked the ability to respond quickly enough to navigate the swiftly changing currents. Even had it had great astuteness, it would have lacked the financial resources to affect significantly the course of events.

In 1962, seven-term Congressman Hugh Addonizio had forged an Italian–Negro coalition to overthrow long-time Irish control of the City Hall. A liberal in Congress, Addonizio, when he became mayor, had opened his door to all people. Negroes, who had been excluded from the previous administration, were brought into the government. The police department was integrated.

Nevertheless, progress was slow. As the Negro population increased, more and more of the politically oriented found the progress inadequate.

The Negro–Italian coalition began to develop strains over the issue of the police. The police were largely Italian, the persons they arrested largely Negro. Community leaders agreed that, as in many police forces, there was a small minority of officers who abused their responsibility. This gave credibility to the cries of "Brutality!" voiced periodically by ghetto Negroes.

In 1965 Mayor Addonizio, acknowledged that there was "a small group of misguided individuals" in the department, declared that "it is vital to establish once and for all, in the minds of the public, that charges of alleged police brutality will be thoroughly investigated and the appropriate legal or punitive action be taken if the charges are found to be substantiated."

Pulled one way by the Negro citizens who wanted a Police Review Board, and the other by the police, who adamantly opposed it, the Mayor decided to transfer "the control and investigation of complaints of police brutality out of the hands of both the police and the public and into the hands of an agency that all can support—the Federal Bureau of Investigation;" and to send "a copy of any charge of police brutality . . . directly to the Prosecutor's office." However, the FBI could act only if there had been a violation of a persons federal civil rights. No complaint was ever heard of again.

Nor was there much redress for other complaints. The city had no money with which to redress them.

The city had already reached its legal bonding limit, yet expenditures continued to outstrip income. Health and welfare costs, per capita, were twenty times as great as for some of the surrounding communities. Cramped by its small land area of 23.6 square miles—one-third of which was taken up by Newark Airport and unusable marshland—and surrounded by independent jurisdictions, the city had nowhere to expand.

·     ·     ·     ·     ·     ·     ·     ·     ·     ·

During the daytime Newark more than doubled its population—and was, therefore, forced to provide services for a large number of people who contributed nothing in property taxes. The city's per capita outlay for police, fire protection and other municipal services continued to increase. By 1967 it was twice that of the surrounding area.

Consequently, there was less money to spend on education. Newark's per capita outlay on schools was considerably less than that of surrounding communities. Yet within the city's school system were 78,000 children, 14,000 more than ten years earlier.

Twenty thousand pupils were on double sessions. The dropout rate was estimated to be as high as 33 per cent. Of 13,600 Negroes between the ages of sixteen and nineteen, more than 6,000 were not in school. In 1960 over half of the adult Negro population had less than an eighth-grade education.

The typical ghetto cycle of high unemployment, family breakup, and crime was present in all its elements. Approximately 12 per cent of Negroes were without jobs. An estimated 40 per cent of Negro children lived in broken homes. Although Newark maintained proportionately the largest police force of any major city, its crime rate was among the highest in the nation. In narcotics violations it ranked fifth nationally. Almost 80 per cent of the crimes were committed within two miles of the core of the city, where the Central Ward is located. A majority of the criminals were Negro. Most of the victims, likewise, were Negro. The Mafia was reputed to control much of the organized crime.

Under such conditions a major segment of the Negro population became increasingly militant. Largely excluded from positions of traditional political power, Negroes, tutored by a handful of militant social activists who had moved into the city in the early 1960's, made use of the anti-poverty program, in which poor people were guaranteed representation, as a political springboard. This led to friction between the United Community Corporation, the agency that administered the anti-poverty program, and the city administration.

When it became known that the secretary of the Board of Education intended to retire, the militants proposed for the position the city's budget director, a Negro with a master's degree in accounting. The Mayor, however, had already nominated a White man. Since the White man had only a high school education, and at least 70 per cent of the children in the school system were Negro, the issue of who was to obtain the secretaryship, an important and powerful position, quickly became a focal issue.

Joined with the issue of the 150-acre medical school site, the area of which had been expanded to triple the original request—an expansion regarded by the militants as an effort to dilute the black political power by moving out Negro residents—the Board of Education battle resulted in a confrontation between the mayor and the militants. Both sides refused to alter their positions.

Into this impasse stepped a Washington Negro named Albert Roy Osborne. A flamboyant, forty-two-year-old former wig salesman who called himself Colonel Hassan Jeru-Ahmed and wore a black beret, he presided over a mythical "Blackman's Volunteer Army of Liberation." Articulate and magnetic, the self-commissioned "Colonel" proved to be a one-man show. He brought Negro residents flocking to Board of Education and Planning Board meetings. The Colonel spoke in violent terms, and backed his words with violent action. At one meeting he tore the tape from the official stenographic recorder. After he was ejected, one of his captains threw a mapboard across the stage and smashed a tape recorder against the wall.

It became more and more evident to the militants that, though they might not be able to prevail, they could prevent the normal transaction of business. Filibustering began. A Negro former state assemblyman held the floor for more than four hours. One meeting of the Board of Education began at 5:00 P.M. and did not adjourn until 3:23 A.M. Throughout the months of May and June speaker after speaker warned that if the Mayor persisted in naming a White man as secretary to the Board of Education, and in moving ahead with plans for the medical school site, violence would ensue. The city administration played down the threats.

On June 27, when a new secretary to the Board of Education was to be named, the state police set up a command post in the Newark armory.

The militants led by the local CORE chapter, disrupted and took over the Board of Education meeting. The outcome was a stalemate. The incumbent secretary decided to stay on another year. No one was satisfied.

At the beginning of July there were 24,000 unemployed Negroes within the city limits. Their ranks were swelled by an estimated 20,000 teenagers, many of whom, with school out and the summer recreation program curtailed due to a lack of funds, had no place to go.

On July 8, Newark and East Orange Police attempted to disperse a group of Black Muslims. In the melee that followed, several police officers and Muslims suffered injuries necessitating medical treatment. The resulting charges and countercharges heightened the tension between police and Negroes.

Early on the evening of July 12, a cab driver named John Smith began, according to police reports, tailgating a Newark police car. Smith was an unlikely candidate to set a riot in motion. Forty years old, a Georgian by birth, he had attended college for a year before entering the Army in 1950. In 1953 he had been honorably discharged with the rank of corporal. A chess-playing trumpet player, he had worked as a musician and a factory hand before, in 1963, becoming a cab driver.

As a cab driver, he appeared to be a hazard. Within a relatively short period of time he had eight or nine accidents. His license was revoked. When, with a woman passenger in his cab, he was stopped by the police, he was in violation of that revocation.

From the high-rise towers of the Reverend William P. Hayes Housing Project, the residents can look down on the orange-red brick facade of the Fourth Precinct Police Station and observe every movement. Shortly after 9:30 P.M., people saw Smith, who either refused or was unable to walk, being dragged out of a police car and into the front door of the station.

Within a few minutes at least two civil-rights leaders received calls from a hysterical woman declaring a cab driver was being beaten by the police. When one of the persons at the station notified the cab company of Smith's arrest, cab drivers all over the city began learning of it over their cab radios.

A crowd formed on the grounds of the housing project across the narrow street from the station. As more and more people arrived, the description of the beating purportedly administered to Smith became more and more exaggerated. The descriptions were supported by other complaints of police malpractice that, over the years, had been submitted for investigation—but had never been heard of again.

Several Negro community leaders, telephoned by a civil-rights worker and informed of the deteriorating situation, rushed to the scene. By 10:15 P.M. the atmosphere had become so potentially explosive that Kenneth Melchior, the senior police inspector on the night watch, was called. He arrived at approximately 10:30 P.M.

Met by a delegation of civil-rights leaders and militants who requested the right to see and interview Smith, Inspector Melchior acceded to their request.

When the delegation was taken to Smith, Melchior agreed with their observations that, as a result of injuries Smith had suffered, he needed to be examined by a doctor. Arrangements were made to have a police car transport him to the hospital.

Both within and outside of the police station the atmosphere was electric with hostility. Carloads of police officers arriving for the 10:45 P.M. change of shifts were subjected to a gauntlet of catcalls, taunts and curses.

Joined by Oliver Lofton, administrative director of the Newark Legal Services Project, the Negro community leaders inside the station requested an interview with Inspector Melchior. As they were talking to the inspector about initiating an investigation to determine how Smith had been injured, the crowd outside became more and more unruly. Two of the Negro spokesmen went outside to attempt to pacify the people.

There was little reaction to the spokesmen's appeal that the people go home. The second of the two had just finished speaking from atop a car when several Molotov cocktails smashed against the wall of the police station.

With the call of "Fire!" most of those inside the station, police officers and civilians alike, rushed out of the front door. The Molotov cocktails had splattered to the ground; the fire was quickly extinguished.

Inspector Melchior had a squad of men form a line across the front of the station. The police officers and the Negroes on the other side of the street exchanged volleys of profanity.

Three of the Negro leaders, Timothy Still of the United Community Corporation, Robert Curvin of CORE, and Lofton, requested they be given another opportunity to disperse the crowd. Inspector Melchior agreed to let them try, and provided a bullhorn. It was apparent that the several hundred persons who had gathered in the street and on the grounds of the housing project were not going to disperse. Therefore, it was decided to attempt to channel the energies of the people into a nonviolent protest. While Lofton promised the crowd that a full investigation would be made of the Smith incident, the other Negro leaders urged those on the scene to form a line of march toward the city hall.

Some persons joined the line of march. Others milled about in the narrow street. From the dark grounds of the housing project came a barrage of rocks. Some of them fell among the crowd. Others hit persons in the line of march. Many smashed the windows of the police station. The rock throwing, it was believed, was the work of youngsters; approximately 2,500 children lived in the housing project.

Almost at the same time, an old car was set afire in a parking lot. The line of march began to disintegrate. The police, their heads protected by World War I-type helmets, sallied forth to disperse the crowd. A fire engine, arriving on the scene, was pelted with rocks. As police drove people away from the station, they scattered in all directions.

A few minutes later a nearby liquor store was broken into. Some persons, seeing a caravan of cabs appear at city hall to protest Smith's arrest, interpreted this as evidence that the disturbance had been organized, and generated rumors to that effect.

However, only a few stores were looted. Within a short period of time disorder ran its course.

The next afternoon, Thursday, July 13, the Mayor described it as an isolated incident. At a meeting with Negro leaders to discuss measures to defuse the situation, he agreed to appoint the first Negro police captain, and announced that he would set up a panel of citizens to investigate the Smith arrest. To one civil-rights leader this sounded like "the playback of a record," and he walked out. Other observers reported that the Mayor seemed unaware of the seriousness of the tensions.

The police were not. Unknown to the Mayor, Dominick Spina, the director of police, had extended shifts from eight hours to twelve, and was in the process of mobilizing half the strength of the department for that evening. The night before, Spina had arrived at the Fourth Precinct Police Station at approximately midnight, and had witnessed the latter half of the disturbance. Earlier in the evening he had held the regular weekly "open house" in his office. This was intended to give any person who wanted to talk to him an opportunity to do so. Not a single person had shown up.

As director of police, Spina had initiated many new programs: police-precinct councils, composed of the police precinct captain and business and civic leaders, who would meet once a month to discuss mutual problems; Junior Crime-fighters; a Boy Scout Explorer program for each precinct; mandatory human relations training for every officer; a Citizens' Observer Program, which permitted citizens to ride in police cars and observe activities in the stations; a Police Cadet program; and others.

Many of the programs initially had been received enthusiastically, but—as was the case with the "open house"—interest had fallen off. In general, the programs failed to reach the hard-core unemployed, the disaffected, the school dropouts—of whom Spina estimates there are 10,000 in Essex County—that constitute a major portion of the police problem.

Reports and rumors, including one that Smith had died, circulated through the Negro community. Tension continued to rise. Nowhere was the tension greater than at the Spirit House, the gathering place for Black Nationalists, Black Power advocates, and militants of every hue. Black Muslims, Orthodox Muslims, and members of the United Afro-American Association, a new and growing organization that follows, in general, the teachings of the late Malcolm X, came regularly to mingle and exchange views. Anti-White playwright LeRoi Jones held workshops. The two police–Negro clashes, coming one on top of the other, coupled with the unresolved political issues, had created a state of crisis.

On Thursday, inflammatory leaflets were circulated in the neighborhoods of the Fourth Precinct. A "Police Brutality Protest Rally" was announced for early evening in front of the Fourth Precinct Station. Several television stations and newspapers sent news teams to interview people. Cameras were set up. A crowd gathered.

A picket line was formed to march in front of the police station. Between 7:00 and 7:30 P.M. James Threatt, executive director of the Newark Human Rights Commission, arrived to announce to the people the decision of the Mayor to form a citizens group to investigate the Smith incident, and to elevate a Negro to the rank of captain.

The response from the loosely milling mass of people was derisive. One youngster shouted "Black Power!" Rocks were thrown at Threatt, a Negro. The barrage of missiles that followed placed the police station under siege.

After the barrage had continued for some minutes, police came out to disperse the crowd. According to witnesses, there was little restraint of language or action by either side. A number of police officers and Negroes were injured.

.    .    .    .    .    .    .    .    .    .

Without the necessary personnel to make mass arrests, police were shooting into the air to clear stores. A Negro boy was wounded by a .22 caliber bullet said to have been fired by a White man riding in a car. Guns were reported stolen from a Sears Roebuck store. Looting, fires, and gunshots were reported from a widening area. Between 2:00 and 2:30 A.M. on Friday, July 14, the mayor decided to request Governor Richard J. Hughes to dispatch the state police, and National Guard troops. The first elements of the state police arrived with a sizeable contingent before dawn.

During the morning the Governor and the Mayor, together with police and National Guard officers, made a reconnaissance of the area. The police escort guarding the officials arrested looters as they went. By early afternoon the National Guard had set up 137 roadblocks, and state police and riot teams were beginning to achieve control. Command of antiriot operations was taken over by the Governor, who decreed a "hard line" in putting down the riot.

As a result of technical difficulties, such as the fact that the city and state police did not operate on the same radio wavelengths, the three-way command structure—city police, state police and National Guard—worked poorly.

At 3:30 P.M. that afternoon, the family of Mrs. D. J. was standing near the upstairs windows of their apartment, watching looters run in and out of a furniture store on Springfield Avenue. Three carloads of police rounded the corner. As the police yelled at the looters, they began running.

The police officers opened fire. A bullet smashed the kitchen window in Mrs. D. J.'s apartment. A moment later she heard a cry from the bedroom. Her three-year-old daughter, Debbie, came running into the room. Blood was streaming down the left side of her face; the bullet had entered her eye. The child spent the next two months in the hospital. She lost the sight of her left eye and the hearing in her left ear.

Simultaneously, on the street below, Horace W. Morris, an associate director of the Washington Urban League who had been visiting relatives in Newark, was about to enter a car for the drive to Newark

Airport. With him were his two brothers and his seventy-three-year-old step-father, Isaac Harrison. About sixty persons had been on the street watching the looting. As the police arrived, three of the looters cut directly in front of the group of spectators. The police fired at the looters. Bullets plowed into the spectators. Everyone began running. As Harrison, followed by the family, headed toward the apartment building in which he lived, a bullet kicked his legs out from under him. Horace Morris lifted him to his feet. Again he fell. Mr. Morris' brother, Virgil, attempted to pick the old man up. As he was doing so, he was hit in the left leg and right forearm. Mr. Morris and his other brother managed to drag the two wounded men into the vestibule of the building, jammed with sixty to seventy frightened, angry Negroes.

Bullets continued to spatter against the walls of the buildings. Finally, as the firing died down, Morris—whose stepfather died that evening—yelled to a sergeant that innocent people were being shot.

"Tell the Black bastards to stop shooting at us," the sergeant, according to Morris, replied.

"They don't have guns; no one is shooting at you," Morris said.

"You shut up, there's a sniper on the roof," the sergeant yelled.

A short time later, at approximately 5:00 P.M., in the same vicinity a police detective was killed by a small caliber bullet. The origin of the shot could not be determined. Later during the riot a fireman was killed by a .30 caliber bullet. Snipers were blamed for the deaths of both.

.     .     .     .     .     .     .     .     .     .

Although, by nightfall, most of the looting and burning had ended, reports of sniper fire increased. The fire was, according to New Jersey National Guard reports, "deliberately or otherwise inaccurate." Major General James F. Cantwell, chief of staff of the New Jersey National Guard, testified before an Armed Services Subcommittee of the House of Representatives that "there was too much firing initially against snipers" because of "confusion when we were finally called on for help and our thinking of it as a military action."

"As a matter of fact," Director of Police Spina told the Commission, "down in the Springfield Avenue area it was so bad that, in my opinion, Guardsmen were firing upon police and police were firing back at them . . . I really don't believe there was as much sniping as we thought . . . We have since compiled statistics indicating that there were seventy-nine specified instances of sniping."

Several problems contributed to the misconceptions regarding snipers: the lack of communications; the fact that one shot might be reported half a dozen times by half a dozen different persons as it caromed and reverberated a mile or more through the city; the fact that the National Guard troops lacked riot training. They were, said a police official, "young and very scared," and had had little contact with Negroes.

.    .    .    .    .    .    .    .    .

By Monday afternoon, July 17, state police and National Guard forces were withdrawn. That evening, a Catholic priest saw two Negro men walking down the street. They were carrying a case of soda and two bags of groceries. An unmarked car with five police officers pulled up beside them. Two white officers got out of the car. Accusing the Negro men of looting, the officers made them put the groceries on the sidewalk, then kicked the bags open, scattering their contents all over the street.

Telling the men, "Get out of here," the officers drove off. The Catholic priest went across the street to help gather up the groceries. One of the men turned to him: "I've just been back from Vietnam two days," he said, "and this is what I get. I feel like going home and getting a rifle and shooting the cops."

Of the 250 fire alarms, many had been false, and thirteen were considered by the city to have been "serious." Of the $10,251,000 damage total, four-fifths was due to stock loss. Damage to buildings and fixtures was less than $2 million.

Twenty-three persons were killed—a white detective, a white fireman, and twenty-one Negroes. One was seventy-three-year-old Isaac Harrison. Six were women. Two were children.

## An American Tragedy—Detroit (1967)*

The trouble burst on Detroit like a firestorm and turned the nation's fifth biggest city into a theater of war. Whole streets lay ravaged by looters, whole blocks immolated in flames. Federal troops—the first sent into racial battle outside the South in a quarter-century—occupied American streets at bayonet point. Patton tanks—machine guns ablaze —and Huey helicopters patroled a cityscape of blackened brick chim-

---

* *Newsweek* (August 7, 1967), 18–27. Copyright Newsweek, Inc. (August, 1967).

neys poking out of gutted basements. And suddenly Harlem 1964 and Watts 1965 and Newark only three weeks ago fell back into the shadows of memory. Detroit was the new benchmark, its rubble a monument to the most devastating race riot in U.S. history—and a symbol of a domestic crisis grown graver than any since the Civil War.

For Detroit's bloody arithmetic—40 deaths, 2,250 injuries, 4,000 arrests, $250 million in property losses—was only the worst of the week's harvest. The fallout struck fire in half a dozen other Michigan cities—in Pontiac and Saginaw, Flint and Grand Rapids, Albion and Kalamazoo. Black-power demagogue Rap Brown invited Negroes to burn down Cambridge, Maryland—and the heart of Cambridge's black quarter shortly went up in flames. The war claimed two lives in Rochester, New York, three in Manhattan's mostly Puerto Rican East Harlem, another in Chicago; it brought the National Guard to Toledo, Ohio, South Bend, Indiana, and Memphis, Tennessee. Rocks and firebombs flew in cities as big as Cincinnati and Cleveland, in suburbs as comfortable as Mount Vernon, New York, and Waukegan, Illinois. No city was safely beyond the battlefield: the homefront war seared thirty cities during the week, perhaps seventy this summer, more than one hundred since the whole deadly cycle began in Harlem three years ago.

And the tragedy was that nobody knew how to stop it—if, indeed, it could be stopped at all. Washington's liberals argued for bigger, more imaginative urban programs—to which the opposition replied that no city has spent poverty money more generously or more energetically than Detroit. Congress, distracted by Vietnam and beset by a bloated budget, was hopping mad over the riots—too angry, in all probability, to do much more than denounce them, investigate them and jam through an "anti-riot" bill that surely could not stop them. Beleaguered Negro moderates pleaded for peace and money—but the fire-eating cries of the Rap Browns seemed to ring louder in the ghetto and on Capitol Hill.

### Poverty

"The mood here is poisonous and self-destructive," said one old Washington hand—and so it seemed as the week's events laid bare a poverty of new ideas. The Republican Party's chief contribution to the crisis dialogue was a policy broadside blaming Mr. Johnson in part for the riots—a screed so partisan that even Senate Minority Leader Ev Dirksen (who read it to the press) conceded privately afterward that it was a bit much. And the President himself was

128    URBAN RACIAL VIOLENCE

scarcely more elevating in a midnight TV speech announcing—after a
long day's vacillation—that he was at last committing United States
paratroopers to battle in Detroit. The point he seemed most eager to
get across was that he had taken that drastic step only after Michigan
Governor George Romney—a potential GOP challenger in 1968—had
confessed himself unable to handle the situation.

But three nights later, an obviously troubled President went back
on TV with an appeal for peace—a nineteen-minute speech that was
assiduously nonpartisan, sometimes eloquent, more often merely
homiletic and largely devoid of any fresh programmatic ideas. He
addressed himself harshly to the rioters: "The violence must be stopped
—quickly, finally and permanently . . . There are no victors in the
aftermath of violence." He scolded a balky Congress for slashing
Great Society programs aimed at the roots of the disorders: "Theirs is
a strange system of bookkeeping." He summoned all Americans to a
happier day "when mercy and truth are met together, righteousness
and peace . . . kiss each other." Yet it was a measure of the depth of
the crisis that Mr. Johnson had, in the end, nothing new to offer except
(1) a national day of prayer; (2) better riot training for National Guard
troops and (3) a bipartisan study commission, headed by Illinois
Governor (and National Guard general) Otto Kerner, to investigate
causes and cures.[1]

Detroit was signal enough that the fire this time could happen
anywhere. The city is the automotive capital of the world; Negroes—
though dogged by an unemployment rate persistently double the
national average—command high wages in the factories and high
positions in the aggressively liberal United Auto Workers union.
Detroit is a homeowners' town as well, and 40 per cent of its 550,000
Blacks own or are buying their own houses—many in integrated neighborhoods. And community leaders, White and Negro, have made a
civics lesson of the ugliest episode in the city's past: the 1943 race riot
that left thirty-four dead and moved Franklin Roosevelt to send in
federal troops. The memory-haunted Detroit Whites learned to deal
with established Negro leaders, and the Black Establishment in turn

---

[1] The other members: New York Mayor John V. Lindsay, vice chairman; United
States Senators Edward Brooke of Massachusetts and Fred R. Harris of Oklahoma;
Congressmen James C. Corman of California and William M. McCulloch of Ohio;
the NAACP's Roy Wilkins; United Steelworkers president I. W. Abel; Charles B.
(Tex) Thornton, chairman of Litton Industries; Kentucky Commerce Commissioner
Katherine Graham Peden; Atlanta Police Chief Herbert Jenkins.

moved into the streets on peacekeeping missions at the slightest stirring of trouble in the ghetto.

And no mayor has been more attentive to the grievances of the hard-core Negro poor than Detroit's Jerome Cavanaugh. He was a bright but obscure lawyer of thirty-three when, in 1961, Negro votes helped elect him mayor over an incumbent widely resented in the ghetto for his scattershot "crackdowns" on crime. Cavanaugh responded by naming liberal police commissioners (first a former state supreme court justice, currently ex-newsman Ray Girardin) and turning the department into a leader in color-sensitive law enforcement. That drew some flak from jittery Whites—crime in the streets is the main issue in a simmering campaign to recall Cavanaugh—but the Mayor held his ground. He lobbied hard and well, moreover, for such federal programs as model cities (which he invented) and anti-poverty (which he has tapped for some $200 million for jobs, job training, education and recreation).

### "The Best"

"Nobody has to throw a brick at City Hall to get our attention," Cavanaugh was fond of saying—yet still the bricks flew. "Detroit is the best city in the world to live in if you're colored," echoed a tack-sharp young Negro who earns $175 a week at Chrysler. "Man, there are just no gripes." Yet he joined in the plunder ("Hell, when you see a broken window and stuff laying all over, anybody will do a little looting") and regretted only the burning that left his street a charred ruin sealed off with military barbed wire.

The spark was the classic one: a trivial police incident. On teeming Twelfth Street, a West Side ghetto strip dominated after dark by hustlers, prostitutes and young hipsters, police mounted a routine 4 A.M. raid on a "blind pig"—an after-hours speakeasy in an abandoned second-floor office. The weather was muggy, the street tense; hours earlier two carloads of Negroes had coursed through whooping, "Unite, Black men! This is a stand! Black Power!" As the blue raiders flushed eighty captives downstairs, knots of Negroes materialized outside, jeering at first, then tossing rocks and bricks at the cops. A brick smashed a cruiser window—a direct hit that turned out be the declaration of war.

### Show the Flag

Precisely at the flashpoint, police made the first in a series of fateful mistakes. They might have pulled out in the hope the crowd would disperse—or they could have moved forward in full force to nip the trouble in the bud. They did neither. Instead, they simply assumed that the Cavanaugh–Girardin walk-soft strategy was in force, spilled cruisers into the area to show the flag but made no effort to beat back the crowd—a decision bitterly denounced by Whites and Negro moderates alike in the aftermath.

The war, as a result, quickly escalated. The emboldened mob spilled garbage into the street and set it afire. Bricks smashed through shop-windows and the looting began. Firebombs flew, and a tepid July breeze fanned the flames. By 6:30, a major blaze erupted in a sacked shoe store—the first of more than 1,500 in the days to come. Cavanagh hustled to a command post at police headquarters, and Romney dispatched an aide to join him, but their first efforts—boggled by sketchy and overly rosy intelligence reports—were embarrassingly inept. Cavanagh ordered extra swimming pools opened. Romney suggested seeding clouds over the ghetto to bring down a cooling rain. And police kept their weapons sheathed; into the evening the mayor was still calling the uprising a "civil disturbance."

It was far more. Looters—some in integrated gangs—ran rampant, smashing windows, picking stores clean, leaving behind them rivers of fire as many as ten blocks long. Shops marked "Soul Brother" or "Afro All the Way" or (as one Negro storekeeper emphatically scrawled) "Very, Very, Very, Very Black" survived until dark—and then fell victim to the thieves. Looters scuttled openly through the streets, loaded down with clothes and food, packing appliances into cars. One White druggist stepped out of his plundered shop and told Negro bystanders: "Take what you want—I'm through." A White grocer found his store picked down to the bare shelves—and calmly set it afire himself.

The atmosphere was almost festive. A crippled man wobbled along with two bottles of whisky in each hand. "Got me some good stuff," he crowed. "I'm gone have me a ball." A teen-ager slithered out of a jewelry store with a gleaming silver teapot. "Whatcha gonna do with that?" a passerby called. "Make me some tea," came the grinning reply. Cavanagh and Romney made one early-morning tour of the ruins, watched some small boys skittering past with liquor bottles tucked under their arms and came back appalled. "People are filled with a carnival spirit," said Cavanagh. "Rioting has become a lark, a joke. There's a sense of euphoria in the air."

The rioters spread through the ghetto and far beyond, etching a trail of fire in their wake. Neither the city's hopelessly outmanned

4,000 cops nor the relays of Negro peacemakers could contain the fury. Democratic United States Representative John Conyers, one of the city's two Negro congressmen, climbed on his car with a "cool-it" speech—and was stoned into retreat. When the Reverend Nicholas Hood, a Negro city councilman, tried his hand, rioters threatened him and his family, and he too evacuated the combat zone.

Finally, Romney moved into the besieged city, proclaimed a state of emergency, clamped down a 9 P.M. curfew and called in state troopers, then the first of some 7,300 National Guardsmen. Where Cavanagh and Girardin had sought merely to contain the rioting, Romney was all for a show of force. Talking strategy with city officials, he recalled "something Ike once told me. He said that when he ran the Normandy invasion there was a great deal of looting at the start. Ike said he ended it by having them catch a looter, shoot him and then hang him up by the heels in the town square ... So let's catch these people right at the start and bring them to court and show them we're tough."

Yet force seemed at first only to fan the flames. The guardsmen particularly proved to be, as they had in Watts and Newark, a ragged, jittery, hair-triggered lot ill-trained in riot control. "We told the men before they moved in here that they're not fighting the Viet Cong— they're fighting their own neighbors." said Guard Major Robert J. Lewis. But one young guardsman, hand trembling on the butt of his M-1 rifle, growled, "I'm gonna shoot anything that moves and is black." Some of his comrades in arms seemed to do precisely that. Tanks strafed buildings indiscriminately in the hunt for snipers. The death toll spiraled. Eight guardsmen stopped a white station wagon in the combat zone, then pumped fourteen shots into it when it started rolling slowly down an incline. One guardsman was wounded. Another fainted. Three bloodied Negroes spilled out into the street; a fourth slumped across the back seat. "There ain't even a goddam penknife in the car," protested one of the Negroes. Said a guardsman: "We didn't know that, pal."

## Paralysis

The rioting raged through the night, and, by morning, Detroit was paralyzed. A pall of smoke hung over much of the city. Sniper fire crackled, and countless burglar alarms clanged eerily. Offices, banks, schools, hotels closed down. Thousands of autoworkers stayed home from the plants. Deliveries were throttled. Food ran short; looters hawked milk for 25 cents a half-gallon and profiteering merchants charged $1 a quart. Two small airlines canceled flights for fear of sniper fire. Thousands of Negro evacuees—some burned out, others frightened away—clogged dozens of refugee centers. Busload after busload of POW's spilled out at jails, and police headquarters was piled high with loot: mod dresses, bongo drums, bananas—and dollies stacked with rifles.

Long before dawn, Romney telephoned United States Attorney General Ramsey Clark to alert him that federal troops might be needed—a call that set off a Kafkaesque eight-hour telephone and telegraph dialogue over the proprieties of legal language. The 1795 law finally invoked by Mr. Johnson authorizes a President to send in troops at the "request" of a governor to put down an "insurrection." Romney left the word "request" out of his first SOS wire; Clark called back to say it had to be included. The AG also wanted the word "insurrection" —but, as Romney heatedly reminded him, insurance companies do not pay off on damage caused by insurrections. "Who's going to rebuild this place after the troops go home?" Romney stormed and slammed down the receiver.

When Romney's formal "request" finally arrived in mid-morning, Mr. Johnson swiftly ordered the Pentagon to start airlifting "Task Force Detroit"—4,700 paratroopers from Fort Bragg, North Carolina, and Fort Campbell, Kentucky—to Detroit's Selfridge Air Force Base, And there they stayed for agonizing hours, forty miles from the combat zone, while the President flew his field team, headed by sometime Deputy Defense Secretary Cyrus Vance, to Detroit for a firsthand look. The Vance party toured the riot-stricken areas, conferred with Romney, Cavanagh and Negro leaders—and concluded incredibly that the troops weren't needed yet.

## Surrender

"We feel it is always best to let the local enforcement officials try to cope with a local situation," Vance insisted—but local officials plainly couldn't cope. Romney was steaming. Cavanagh, normally nerveless, told Vance icily: "I don't want to be an ungrateful host but it is my position that we should have the commitment of federal troops at this time." Congressman Charles Diggs Jr., a Negro, called the White House to demand troops; so did the UAW's Walter Reuther. Finally, Vance—and the President—conceded. Vance shuttled 1,800 troops to a fairgrounds at the edge of town by 10:30 P.M., moved them into the East Side ghetto three hours later.

Even then, in his midnight TV message, the President chose gracelessly to mention Republican Romney thirteen times, Democrat

Cavanagh only twice. "Law and order have broken down in Detroit,"
he said. Mr. Johnson acted "only because of the clear, unmistakable
and undisputed evidence that Governor Romney of Michigan and the
local officials . . . have been unable to bring the situation under control."
"That isn't right," said Romney as an aide flicked off his TV set.
"Here I've been working all day and he lays it onto me like that."
Next day, jaw set and eyes frosty, he snapped: "As far as I'm concerned,
the President played politics with a riot."

But the President's troops, once they got into action, played hob
with the rioters. Their commandant, Lieutenant-General John L.
Throckmorton, a ribbon-chested ramrod-backed professional who
served as William Westmoreland's deputy in Vietnam, divided the
city down Woodward Avenue, took the eastern sector for his men, left
the West Side to guardsmen and police. In sharp contrast to the Guard,
Throckmorton's well-trained and well-disciplined men—many of them
blooded in Vietnam and the Dominican Republic—packed only small
arms (M-16 rifles, grenade launchers, tear gas) and steady trigger
fingers. While the Guard's machine guns chopped randomly at building
fronts, the paratroopers isolated real snipers' nests, stalked them with
deadly, dogged accuracy and quickly pacified the East Side. "I've
been in the D.R. [Dominican Republic]," said one sergeant, "and I
know a little about this house-to-house fighting."

But the advent of the federal troops only shifted the locus of war
back to the West Side, where it all began. At its boiling peak, the riot
had spread over fourteen square miles of the city, flared in the enclaves
of Hamtramck and Highland Park, penetrated the downtown business
district and reached perilously close to the fashionable Grosse Pointe
suburbs. But now it receded back to Detroit's poorest, angriest sur-
viving ghetto at the city's center, and it took on the chilling cast of
guerrilla warfare.

### Desperadoes

Snipers operating singly or in teams aimed spanging potshots at
firemen, laid siege to precinct police stations, shot and killed a White
woman watching the riot from her motel window. There were no more
than one hundred in all, some of them organized in nationalist or
terrorist cells ("We're as organized as the Viet Cong, baby," boasted
one combatant), others simply the bitterest of the ghetto's honky-hating
spiritual desperadoes. "I popped me some peckerwoods last night,
man, and I'm gone get some mo' tonight," boasted one streetcorner
hanger-on. "I got me three shotguns last night, and I bought a tommy

gun three months ago in Cleveland." And some were White terrorists improbably allied with the Negroes.

The National Guard—and the police—countered with their own clumsy search-and-destroy operation. A badly scared Pfc. wobbled off Twelfth Street shouting about his colleagues, "They're killing anything that moves." A huge M-48 tank lumbered in like a big black ghost, its guns powdering the front of a red-brick building for twenty-five minutes. Police moved in afterward, found a family of four huddled in terror under the back porch, the two children crying hysterically. The sniper—if there was one—disappeared. Police answering a sniper call strafed the Algiers Motel, later moved in, found three dead Negroes —and no guns. At a street crossing, guardsmen spotted two Negro men in a Chevy convertible cruising up Mack Avenue. A dozen cops and guardsmen fanned out in the street. The car slowed, hesitated, then swung left and picked up speed. "Get him!" someone shouted. There was a volley of shots; the Negro in the passenger seat slumped dead, blood oozing from his back. There were no weapons to be found in the car.

Peace

In the end, the riot burned itself out. By the weekend, the curfew had been lifted once, then reimposed as a check not on snipers but on sightseers. On Twelfth Street, a bedsheet fluttered from a third-floor window with a scrawled prayer. "Peace On Earth." The ghetto mopped up its rubble, hosed down its last smoldering fires and buried its dead: all but eight of the fatalities were Negroes—and three of the Whites had been shot as suspected rioters. And so, in the end, it was the Negroes who paid the heaviest price.

It was the revolt of the underground, tragically far beyond the ken of most Whites and many middle-class Negroes. In a crisis mood, four top leaders of the Negro establishment—the NAACP's Wilkins, the Urban League's Whitney Young, Martin Luther King and trade union elder A. Philip Randolph—put together a statement decrying the riots: "Killing, arson, looting are criminal acts and should be dealt with as such ... We are confidant that the overwhelming majority of the Negro community joins us in opposition to violence in the streets." But they were the old soldiers of the Negro revolt; the cruel irony of their position today was that the very victories they had won had only quickened Negro hopes—not satisfied them. Revolts are born of hope, not utter despair, and they quickly cast aside those leaders who seem unable to keep the pace. King recognized the point when someone suggested that he go to Detroit. "I am not a fireman," he said. "My role is keeping fires from starting."

A revolution produces its own Jacobins as well, and the Jacobins of the ghetto are the Stokely Carmichaels and the Rap Browns with their seductive anthems of violence. They exalt riots into rebellions; they bait the "honkies" in ever more extravagant terms; they once read Camus but now their saints are Malcolm X and Frantz Fanon, a Black psychiatrist who concluded from a sojourn among Algerian rebels that violence is therapeutic for Black colonials. Stokely was in Cuba last week [July 30], titillating the Castro press with talk of a developing United States Black guerrilla movement and nominating Detroit and New York as future Vietnams. And Brown, who succeeded Carmichael as chairman of the Student Nonviolent Coordinating Committee, trumpeted: "If you give me a gun and tell me to shoot my enemy, I might shoot Lady Bird!"

From their flamboyant behavior, the easy judgment—and a common one around Capitol Hill—was that all the rioting was part of some master conspiracy. The Justice Department, with its access to FBI intelligence data, insisted there was no evidence of a conspiracy (though there was some evidence of organization among small guerrilla cadres once the riot began). Detroit's police chief Girardin quite agreed: he thought some of the snipers were organized, but the riot itself seemed to him the spontaneous uprising of "rebels with a vague cause." Yet the devil theory still haunted the Hill. It lay behind the mounting demands for a Congressional investigation, and it pervaded the GOP Coordinating Committee statement—a florid picture of Molotov-cocktail factories and national riot-planning meetings (painted largely, as it turned out, by principal author Tom Dewey from accounts he had read in the papers).

That document was still more notable for its blistering assault on Mr. Johnson. It pictured the United States as "rapidly approaching a state of anarchy" and castigated the President for having "totally failed to recognize the problem . . ." [and] vetoed legislation and opposed other legislation designed to re-establish peace and order." The vetoed measure turned out to be the 1966 District of Columbia crime bill— a bill of dubious constitutionality and questionable relevance to Detroit or Newark—and the "other legislation" was the "anti-riot" bill (which Mr. Johnson has neither endorsed nor opposed). Democrats sourly dubbed the statement's authors the "Republican Non-violent Co-ordinating Committee"—and, though it issued from the party's top policy council, a good many GOP moderates disowned it. "Irresponsible," thundered Kentucky's Senator Thruston Morton, an ex-GOP National Chairman. He called on the GOP to "get out of this political arena" and fund a $1 billion "antiriot chest" for the ghettos.

But even Lyndon Johnson vowed on television that there would be "no bonus" for rioters, and, to this angry Congress, any measure to put money into the Black slums looked like a reward for hooliganism. The House, as the President pointedly noted, had already cut expenditures for model cities, the Teachers Corps, rent subsidies and aid to education—and turned down even a meager $40 million for rat control.

## Mood

"There are those who would have us turn back even now, at the beginning of this journey," Mr. Johnson said. "This is not a time for angry reaction . . . It is a time for . . . legislative action to improve the life in our cities." But angry reaction was a catching mood on the Hill and particularly in the House. The spirit of the day was to treat the riots chiefly as a law-enforcement problem, a tide that may carry LBJ's "safe streets" bill (which provides $50 million support for local police) and a gun-control measure but spells trouble for social legislation.

And that promised to be a singularly lopsided legislative track. One lesson of Detroit was not that poverty and welfare programs are irrelevant but that they are, as presently constituted, simply not enough. For this, the President shares the responsibility with Congress. He had preshrunk his programs to help cover the costs of a more distant conflict in Vietnam; the original battle plan for his war on poverty programmed $4 billion for this year, but he asked for only $2 billion and will be lucky to get even that. Illinois's Republican Senator Charles Percy, for one, questions his fiscal arithmetic: "If we continue to spend $66 million a day trying to 'save' the 16 million people of South Vietnam, while leaving the plight of the 20 million urban poor in our own country unresolved, then I think we have our priorities terribly confused." And even some Administration topsiders think any recipe for peace must include a good deal more money—and a good deal more presidential leadership as well.

## Inquiry

Yet another lesson of Detroit was how little America had learned in four long, hot summers about what makes a riot—let alone how to prevent or control one. Stealing the march on several eager congressional committees, Mr. Johnson took just six hours to put his own commission of inquiry together and thirty-six more to get it working in Washington. There, he framed a set of questions: How do riots start? Why do they happen in some cities and not others? Are they organized? How can the law best snuff them out? How can the government best get at the underlying grievances that provoke them? He asked an interim report by March 1, final recommendations in a year. The task was enormous. "We are being asked," said chairman [Otto] Kerner, "to probe into the soul of America."

A man must choose sides, Albert Camus wrote in "The Plague," between the pestilence and its victims. The pestilence in America last week was not only the violent rioting but the conditions that fed it; the victims, in the end, were all Americans, White and Black. It was this distinction Lyndon Johnson grappled with, incompletely and ambivalently, in his second TV report to a troubled nation. "We have endured a week," he said, "such as no nation should live through; a time of violence and tragedy." The violence must and would be stopped, he said, but it would "compound the tragedy . . . if we should settle for order that's imposed by the muzzle of a gun . . . The only genuine, long-range solution for what has happened lies in an attack— mounted at every level—upon the conditions that breed despair and breed violence . . . We should attack these problems not because we are frightened by conflict but because we are fired by conscience." It remained to be seen whether the fire within could burn as strongly as the fire in the streets.

# Chapter Seven

# A Consensus of Attitudes

The riots of the 1960's can be interpreted as an exercise of will, the emergence of solidarity, of group consciousness *to be*. In this regard we can explore the consensus of attitudes among ghetto residents towards American society at large. That the minorities expressed their hostilities in violent ways demonstrated the failure of society to enable the non-White have-nots to participate as equals in our democratic nation. Consequently, there rose up in the core area of the nation's cities a cry of protest which was remarkably of the same tenor and resonance.

## Violence in the Ghettos (1968)*

*Joseph Boskin*

Writing about the implications of the abolition of slavery in the South in the 1830's, Alexis de Tocqueville, in his inimical, incisive manner, observed:

---

* Reprinted from the *New Mexico Quarterly*, XXVII (Winter, 1968), 317–333, with deletions.

I am obliged to confess that I do not regard the abolition of
slavery as a means of warding off the struggle of the two races.
. . . The Negroes may long remain slaves without complaining;
but if they are once raised to the level of freemen, they will soon
revolt at being deprived of almost all of their civil rights; and
as they cannot become the equals of the Whites, they will speedily
show themselves as enemies.[1]

The revolt of the inner-city Negro in the 1960's reflects the failure
of American society effectively to cope with the gap between the
Negroes' racial environment and the ideals of American democracy.
To have developed a series of programs which would narrow the
discrepancies between reality and ideal, however, would have neces-
sitated an understanding of the meaning of Black ghetto life. In
retrospect, it is clear that the lack of a basic comprehension on the
part of the Caucasian with Negro life contributed heavily to the mass
violence in the urban areas. Indeed, it continues to be a factor in the
growing polarization of the two racial groups, despite the best inten-
tions of various individuals and organizations to prevent it.

Perhaps the readiest indication of the Caucasian's blind spot has
been his inability to grasp the message of the mass rioting and to deal
with it in any terms but that of Negro lawlessness or primitiveness.
Former Los Angeles Chief of Police William H. Parker, a representative
spokesman for his counterparts, likened the Negroes of the Watts
Riots to "monkeys in a zoo."[2]

Criticism of the riots was also voiced by some elements of the
Negro community. While not using such prejudicial phrases, they
argued that the riots would increase White backlash and undercut the
Civil Rights Movement, with the result that White–Black relations
would revert to the pre-World War II period. Ignored by both groups
is the fact that violence has been an expression of anger as well as of
hope.

The riots reveal a commonality of purpose among their participants,
active and inactive. The opening riots of 1964–65 may have been
more spontaneous in that they had no antecedents; yet the riots of
1966–67 were remarkably alike in their causes, developments, and
adherents. Several discernible patterns lead to the hypothesis that

---

[1] Alexis de Tocqueville, *Democracy in America*, I (New York: Vintage Books, 1945),
p. 394.

[2] *Newsweek* (August 30, 1965), 5.

there existed among Negroes an antagonism to their environment which produced a consensus for violence. The continuity of behavior of the various riots, the focus of discontent, the modes of antagonism, the directive force, the composition of the rioters, and the milieu of the ghetto converged to create a commonality of purpose among Negroes.

The basis of this consensus for violence, the perspective of ghetto life which escapes the grasp of the Caucasian, can be summed up in the analogy of the ghetto as a colonial region. This analogy is the theme of several works. Kenneth Clark in *Dark Ghetto* maintains that the Negro urban community is similar in status and in problems to that of a colony:

> The dark ghettos are social, political, educational, and—above all — economic colonies. Their inhabitants are subject peoples, victims of the greed, cruelty, insensitivity, guilt, and fear of their masters.[3]

The analogy is extended in *Black Power*, written by Stokely Carmichael, who is associated with the contemporary usage of the phrase, and by Charles V. Hamilton, a sociologist. They argue that the "Black people in this country form a colony, and it is not in the interest of the colonial power to liberate them."[4] Recognizing that the analogy departs from a strict definition of colonialism, nevertheless Carmichael and Hamilton maintain that—

> It is the objective relationship which counts, not rhetoric (such as constitutions *articulating* equal rights) or geography. . . . Black people in the United States have a colonial relationship to the larger society, a relationship characterized by institutional racism.[5]

The basic failures of the Western powers in the developing nations both in Africa and in Asia can also apply to the ghetto. Fred R. Von de Mehden outlines three important areas of neglect: 1) the paternalistic attitude of the colonial powers which "did not foster self-reliance in the native population," 2) the failure of the colonial

---

[3] Kenneth Clark, *Dark Ghetto* (New York: Harper & Row, 1965), p. 11.

[4] Stokely Carmichael and Charles V. Hamilton, *Black Power: The Politics of Liberation in America* (New York: Random House, 1967), p. 5.

[5] *Ibid.*, p. 6.

power to provide adequate education and training for members of the native population to assume positions that had been filled by European citizens, and 3) economic policies of the colonial power which exploited the natural and human resources of the colony.[6]

Colonialism produces certain psychological affects which can be observed in the behavior of natives of colonial regions and of Negroes in the ghettos. The impairment of self-worth is a direct consequence of overlordship. The relationship of the ruling group to the under-advantaged is pervasively demeaning on all levels. Lucien W. Pye thus explains the colonial peoples' "disturbing doubts about the worth of self":

> The seeds of such doubts were, of course, planted by the mechan-
> ics of colonialism, which inescapably cast one people in the role
> of superior and the other in the role of inferior. Moreover, the
> master peoples usually drove their point home with permanent
> effect by employing either consciously or unconsciously all the
> thousand and one techniques and tricks by which most elites
> throughout time have sought to demonstrate their natural rights
> of mastership and to unnerve and demoralize the common people.[7]

Racism, and its prime form of expression, segregation, has produced the identical psychological heritage of Negro self-abnegation. "Human beings who are forced to live under ghetto conditions," observes Kenneth Clark, "and whose daily experience tells them that almost nowhere in society are they respected and granted the ordinary dignity and courtesy accorded to others will, as a matter of course, begin to doubt their own worth."[8]

A second manifestation of the racially underprivileged is a sense of alienation. Denied the possibility of assimilating into Caucasian society either through the occupational door or the split-level, middle-income door; forced to attend substandard, segregated schools; ignored in the history books of the country in which they had worked and lived; associated with the slave, inferior positions of the past; referred to in demeaning terms as "nigger," "boy," or "jungle-bunnies"; and simply

---

[6] Fred R. Von der Mehden, *Politics of the Developing Nations* (Englewood Cliffs: Prentice-Hall, Inc., 1964), pp. 22–26.

[7] Lucien W. Pye, *Politics, Personality, and Nation Building* (New Haven: Yale University Press, 1962), p. 9.

[8] Clark, *op. cit.*, pp. 63–64.

ignored, the Negro has been the rejected man of American society. Cast out of English colonial society in the seventeenth century, the Negro has remained *the* outsider. It was to be expected that his feelings of rejection would produce not only self-doubt but hatred of the oppressor. A Negro youth in Detroit expressed these dual feelings during the summer of the riot:

> You know what I learned in school, man? I learned Paul Revere, who was white, and Christopher Columbus, who was white, and Cleopatra — they said she was white, too. And oh yes, don't forget Little Black Sambo! The Irish had a culture, everybody had a culture, but they told us the Black man's culture was picking more cotton than the white man. That won't do. If it's only a jungle culture, then let's have a jungle culture. I may be flat-nosed, kinky-haired, black as sin and big-assed, but I'm a man, and I can knock your block loose.[9]

Frustration, hatred and the urge to retaliate have long been recognized as a smoldering constant in subjugated groups—Negro American or native. Evidence of aggression by individuals and groups in the Old South is abundant; similarly, evidence of retaliation by native groups is equally abundant. However, the basic question as to why the riots occurred in the cities in the 1960's is crucial to an understanding of the ambience of violence. Significantly, in the period following World War II, many African nations gained their independence from colonial control. The concept of self-determination bore the logical fruit of seeds planted by the American Revolution. The connection between the two events could be seen on the scribbled quotations from the Declaration of Independence and Gettysburg Address on Batavian buildings, penned by nationalistic Indonesians against the Dutch.[10]

Whereas the postwar period signaled the protest of colonial peoples against the ruling countries, the Civil Rights Movement of the 1950's and 1960's heralded the protest of Negroes against the hierarchy in the American South. It is significant that the actions of an unknown seamstress, Rosa Parks, who refused to move to the back of the bus

---

[9] J. Anthony Lukas, "Postscript on Detroit: 'Whitey Hasn't Got the Message,' " *New York Times Magazine* (August 27, 1967), 56.

[10] Carl Degler, *Out of Our Past* (New York: Harper & Row, 1959), p. 104.

in Montgomery, Alabama, triggered the massive protest against the Jim Crow regulations in that city.

The actions of the four North Carolina Agricultural College students who devised and initiated the sit-in protest at the Kresge department store in Greensboro in 1960 were reflective of the changed consicousness which had occurred in the young Negro. Moreover, the rapidity with which the Civil Rights Movement developed, the creativity of its techniques, the acceptance of verbal and physical assault and jailings, the revitalization of CORE and the establishment of SNCC as prime civil-rights organizations, all point to the growing consensus for action and the tough-mindedness of the Negro.

The convergent result in both the emerging nations and in the Negro, whether in the urban ghetto or rural hamlet, has been the attempt to recreate a positive, historical image of Self. The victim of subjugation can rarely escape from the self-conception of inferiority without first building a new image of himself that offers self-respect and dignity. "Each national group ... has reacted strongly and, to some extent, defensively to charges of inferiority. Each has demanded a sense of dignity and a feeling of worth."[11] Thus the Negro American and the peoples of formerly colonial territories have begun to reexamine their past heritage and to develop techniques of creating self-worth. It is extremely interesting to note that the title of one of the important works in this area by Essien-Udom, *Black Nationalism*, is subtitled "A Search for Identity in America,"[12] and Pye's study *Politics, Personality, and Nation Building* is subheaded "Burma's Search for Identity."

In the forefront of the Negro American struggle to develop a positive identity have been the nationalist movements, the most widely publicized being the [Black] Muslims. This latter movement has been limited to the lower socioeconomic classes and has thus far achieved relatively little influence or support from the urban Negro. Several other organizations have emerged to unite in giving voice to the cry of "Black Power." Imprecise and controversial in its meaning, yet explicit in its implications, "Black Power" expresses the spirit of the young contemporary Negro. The furor created by its usage appears to stem from the word "black." Had Stokely Carmichael called for "Negro Power" during the Meredith March, few objections would have been heard.

---

11 Thomas F. Pettigrew, *A Profile of the Negro American* (Princeton: D. Van Nostrand Co., 1964), p. xii.

12 Essien-Udom, *Black Nationalism* (New York: Dell Publishing Co., 1962), p. 17.

That this would appear to be the situation is indicated by the antecedents of the phrase. Lerone Bennett, Jr., in his book *Before the Mayflower*[13] and in his *Ebony* magazine series, "Black Power," used it without notice. Loren Miller, at the time of his vice-presidency of the National Association for the Advancement of Colored People, made reference to a vital aspect of the concept of Black Power when he wrote in a widely read article: "To liberals a fond farewell, with thanks for services rendered, until you are ready to re-enlist as foot soldiers and subordinates in a Negro-led, Negro-officered army under the banner of Freedom Now."[14] This statement was reprinted and distributed by the NAACP in 1962. In recent years, Congressman Adam Clayton Powell and Floyd McKissick of the Congress of Racial Equality have made frequent use of the term. There was little reaction either to the phrase or to its antecedents until Stokely Carmichael extolled it passionately to rally a group of protest marchers and sharecroppers in the Meredith March in Mississippi.

The word "black" however, evokes many psychological images to Caucasians, images which frequently connote fearful consequences. More, it suggests a usurpation of power and possession. In the context of the relationship between the colonist or settler and the colonized people this fear has considerable validity. Franz Fanon in his powerful book, *The Wretched of the Earth*, describes the unspoken tension which exists between the two groups:

> The look that the native turns on the settler's town is a look of lust, a look of envy; it expresses his dreams of possession — all manner of possession: to sit at the settler's table, to sleep in the settler's bed, with his wife if possible. The colonized man is an envious man. And this the settler knows very well; when their glances meet he ascertains bitterly, always on the defensive "They want to take our place." It is true, for there is no native who does not dream at least once a day of setting himself up in the settler's place.[15]

Despite the absence of a concise definition of "Black Power" in American society, its message is a powerful assertion of self-pride and

[13] Lerone Bennett, Jr., *Before the Mayflower* (Chicago: Johnson Publishing Co., n. d.).

[14] "Farewell to Liberals: A Negro View," *The Nation* (October 20, 1962), 238.

[15] Franz Fanon, *The Wretched of the Earth* (New York: Grove Press, Inc., 1963), p. 32.

self-belief. This feeling has been enhanced by the phrase "black is beautiful." Both phrases reject the centuries of denial of dignity.

The accent on the word "black" also derives from another aspect of the alienation of the Negro in the contemporary period, namely, the failure of society to narrow the gap between expectations and fulfillment. Contrast of White and Negro levels of living is extremely important. Exclaimed a young Negro to writer Budd Schulberg in the Watts Happening Coffee Shop after the riot:

> Drive out of Watts, go north and west and it's beginning to look like the El Dorado those Conquistadores were always hunting for. You've conquered it, baby. Groovy. You've got it made. Some night on the roof of our rotten, falling-down buildings we can actually see your lights shining in the distance. So near and yet so far. We want to reach out and grab it and punch it on the nose.[17]

The inclination to draw comparisons with those Negroes who have "succeeded" adds further frustration. A Detroit Negro schoolteacher observed after the riot of 1967: "The cat on Twelfth Street can look a hundred yards away and see another Black cat living in an eight-room house with a 1967 Pontiac and a motorboat on Lake Michigan." Quickly, however, he returned to the different socioeconomic levels between Negroes and Caucasians:

> . . . General Motors itself is only a few blocks away. I've seen kids from my school walk over to the showroom and sit down in a new model Cadillac, sort of snuggle their little rear ends into the soft leather, slide their hands over the slick plastic steering wheel and say, "Man, I feel that." It's all so far away, and the frustrations just eat them up.[18]

Contrast between the hopeful objectives of the poverty programs and their actual accomplishment is another aspect of the dashed expectations. "To raise the level of expectations without providing corresponding opportunity is psychologically devasting," said George Henderson, a Negro assistant to the superintendent of the Detroit

---

[17] Budd Schulberg, "Watts Riots—End or Beginning?" *Los Angeles Times* (May 15, 1966), *Opinion*, 3.

[18] Lukas, *op. cit.*, 41.

public schools.[19] The parallel between the lives of subject peoples and the colonial authorities can be made here as well. Setting themselves apart from the natives, living in noticeably larger houses and estates, travelling in automobiles, the colonials created such an insufferable contrast as to cause rioting natives in many African nations to destroy houses and estates in the turbulent period of the 1950's and 1960's.

Thus the colonial heritage of subjugation and the Negroes' history of ghetto experience are comparable in that each produced a desperate need to alter individual and group identity and to make the potentials of "mother country" their own as well. In one case this driving need led to nationalistic upheavals, in the other case to the explosion of urban riots.

. . . . . . . . . . .

The explosion in the Black ghettos, like the uprisings of the nationalistic groups in the colonial regions, was the observable expression of a consonance of feeling which developed as a consequence of historical and ecological forces. There has been yet another influence, external to the immediate experience of the urban Negro but supportive of his protest. Massive protest movements on almost all levels of American society have been one of the main characteristics of the decade of the 1960's. Protest groups have been active in secular and nonsecular universities and colleges; in high schools via "underground" newspapers; in the middle classes by such groups as the hippies; in the organizations of other ethnic groups such as Mexican-American and Japanese-American; in the rise of "outsider" newspapers such as the *Free Press* and political journals such as *Ramparts;* in the rise of the New Left; in the anti-Vietnam and anti-Draft Movements. The protest of the contemporary period has been synonomous with the younger generation whose energy has been given to action rather than to ideology. The riots of the Negro, therefore, and to a lesser extent the Puerto Rican, are in keeping with the protest of the present. They have become, however, a protest of violence.

. . . . . . . . . . .

Thus the rioters signaled the significance of the riots. "This is where our calendar starts." . . . "We made Whitey sit up and take notice." Exclaimed a young Negro man at a youth symposium in the Negro district of Oakland, California: "Many Negroes would rather

---

[19] *Ibid.*, 43.

die than live under conditions as they are now. For these people, riots present the only chance of ever achieving equality."[20] As an unemployed youth at a street-corner meeting in Watts after the riot told Bayard Rustin, "We won." Rustin asked dubiously: "How have you won? Homes have been destroyed. Negroes are lying dead in the streets, the stores from which you buy food and clothes are destroyed, and people are bringing you relief." The reply was assertive: "We won because we made the world pay attention to us. The Police Chief never came before; the Mayor always stayed uptown. We made them come."[21]

The riots were an emotionally liberating and identifying event in the lives of contemporary Negroes. Many commentators have noted the "carnival" atmosphere, the unrestrained joy on the faces of the Negroes participating in the event. Similar to the cry of "Black Power," the riots have

> forged a new sense of identity. The riots welded them together, and now they feel capable of serving a new fate, not just passively enduring their present existence. Perhaps every national and racial identity derives from the fact — or at least the legend — of aggressive rising. Is not every revolution a sudden and abrupt break with the past and the potential beginning of a new tradition?[22]

The thirty-one riots which raged in the cities from 1964 to 1967 must be viewed within the context of a consensus on the part of Negroes to gain dignity, status and power within American society in a manner similar to the attempts of the newly emerging Black nations. Further, the riots can be said to have been an integral aspect of the protest of the 1960's. Although having become protests of retaliative violence, they represent an expression of the Civil Rights and other Negro movements. The ultimate objective of these movements is to introduce revolutionary change within the framework of the American social and political structure. Alexis de Tocqueville noted over a century ago:

> If ever America undergoes great revolutions, they will be brought about by the presence of the black race on the soil of the United States; that is to say, they will owe their origin, not to the equality, but to the inequality of condition.[23]

[20] "Youth Discusses Racial Problems," *Human Relations News*, Alameda, California, I (September, 1967).

[21] "The Watts 'Manifesto' and the McCone Report," *Commentary* (March, 1966), 30.

[22] Frederic J. Hacker and Aljean Harmetz, "What the McCone Commission Didn't See," *Frontier Magazine* (March, 1966), 13.

[23] De Tocqueville, *Democracy in America*, II (New York: Vintage Books, 1945), p. 270.